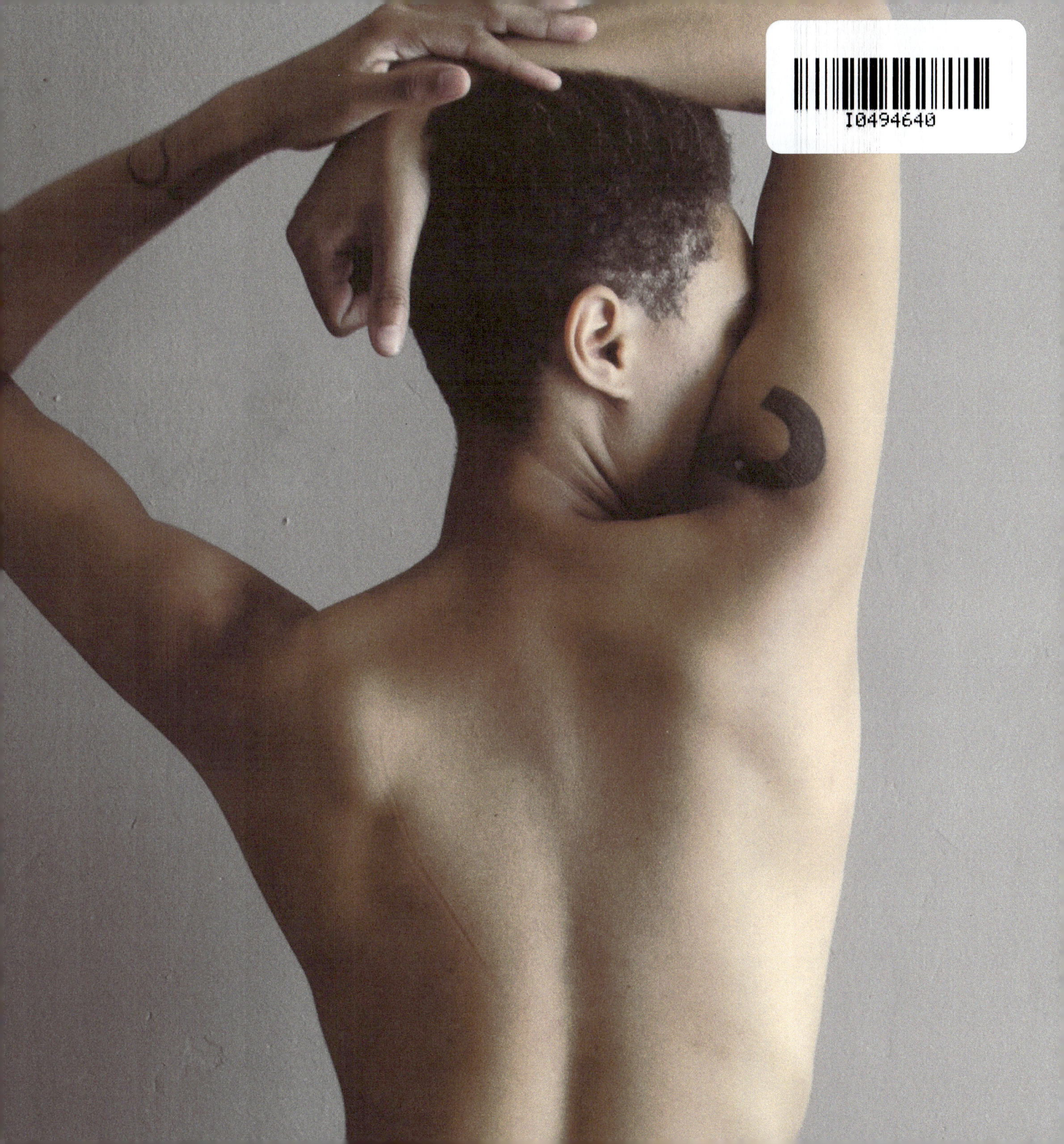

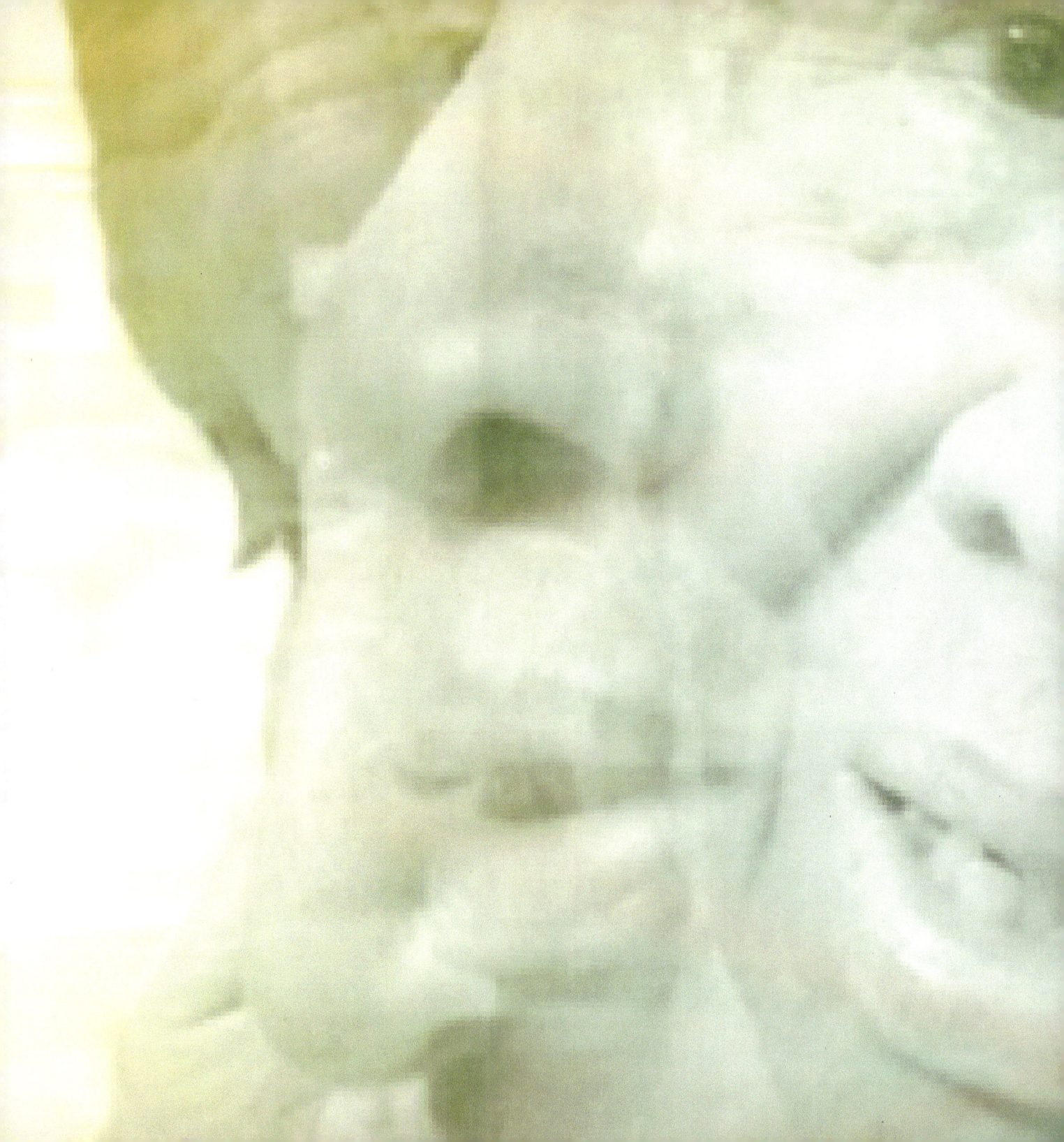

I, Be. I, Be. I, Be. I, Be. I, Be. I, Be.
I, Be. I, Be. I, Be. I, Be. I, Be. I, Be.
I, Be. I, Be. I, Be. I, Be. I, Be. I, Be.

c o n t r i b u t o r s

Brandon Breaux
Myia N. Brown
Lee Bullitt
David Anthony Geary
Brian Dovie Golden
Daniel Gamez

Debra Livingston
Victoria Selbach
Saba Taj
Martha Wade
Guanyu Xu
Reisha

"I, Be." a *PoetsArtists* Exhibition Curated by Janice Bond
Opens September 16th at Elephant Room Gallery in Bridgeport

Elephant Room Gallery is excited to be working with *PoetsArtists* on a portrait exhibition curated by multidisciplinary curator Janice Bond entitled, "I. Be". This exhibition features portrait work in a variety of mediums by artists from all over world. Exhibiting artists include Brandon Breaux, Myia N. Brown, Lee Bullitt, David Anthony Geary, Brian Dovie Golden, Daniel Gamez, Debra Livingston, Victoria Selbach, Saba Taj, Martha Wade, Guanyu Xu and Reisha.

"The works featured in I, Be are equally astounding in technique as they are strong personal reflections of the artist. Both collectors and artists will sincerely appreciate this exhibition." - Kimberly L. Atwood, Owner/Curator of Elephant Room Gallery.

Curator's Statement

"Identity is both the lens and filter by which we see and experience ourselves. Although variables such as gender, popular culture, environment, and heritage may inform how one initially constructs a sense of who they are, time and experience naturally evolves this initial imprint into a more complex structure. How does this internal "portrait" of oneself affect the way we process our lives, society, and our families? How does it affect our rate of consumption, our health, and our safety?

Highlighting the multiple dimensions and narratives that determine and influence our personal, political, and social self-awareness, identity resurfaces in truth as more than simply an internal or external dialogue by which we govern ourselves. It is the key platform by which we reveal determine a sense of place, power, and most importantly, peace." - Janice Bond

"I, Be" opens on Friday, September 16th with a reception open to the public from 6:00pm to 9:00pm at Elephant Room Gallery's Bridgeport location - 2727 S Mary St. in Chicago. The exhibition runs through October 29th and features an Artist Discussion on Sunday, October 16th at 2pm. Viewings are available by appointment and additional open hours can be found on the gallery's website: elephantroomgallery.com

Debra Livingston

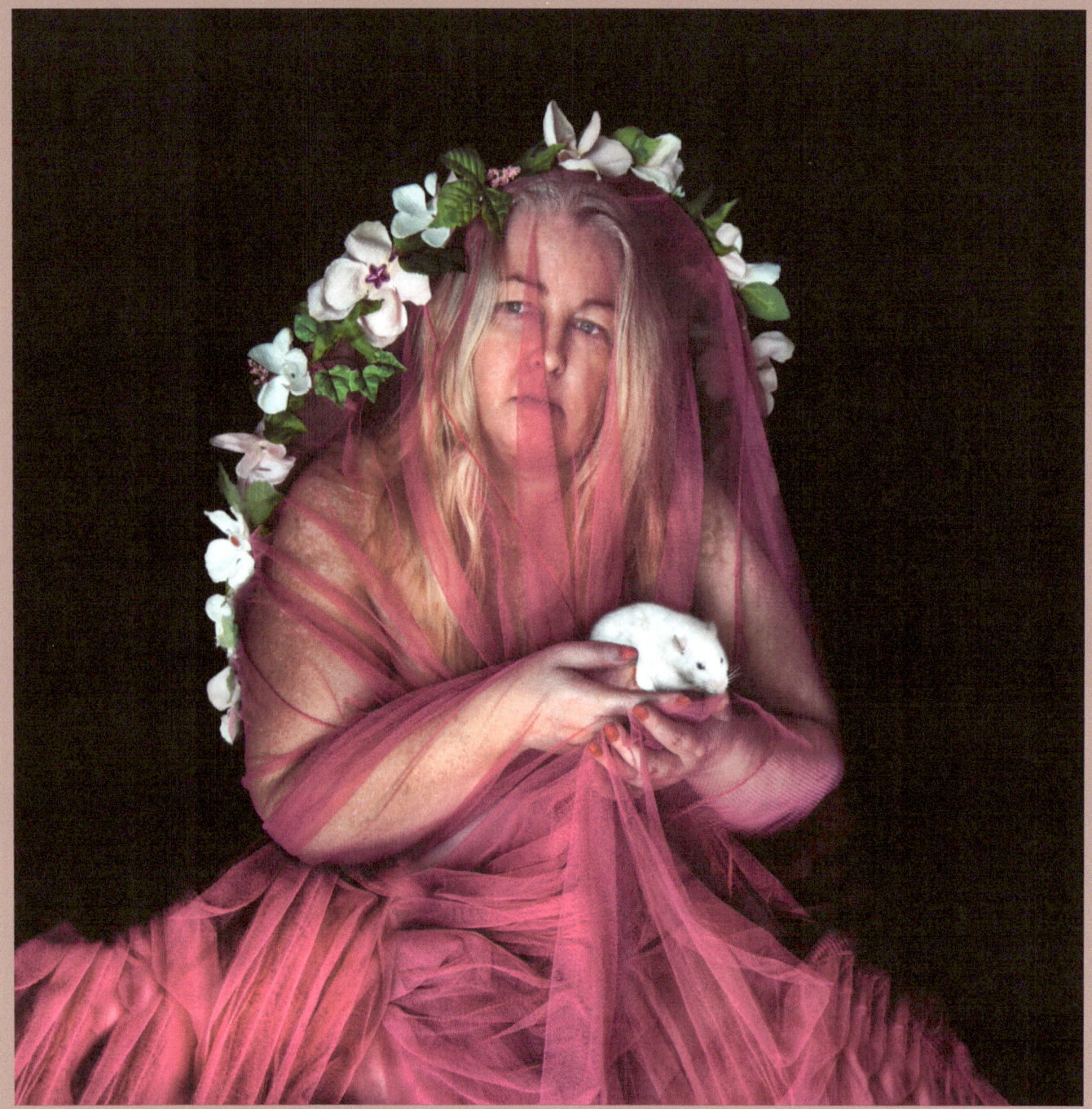

Princess Leah Rose 1 and 2 | Photography | 35 inches square

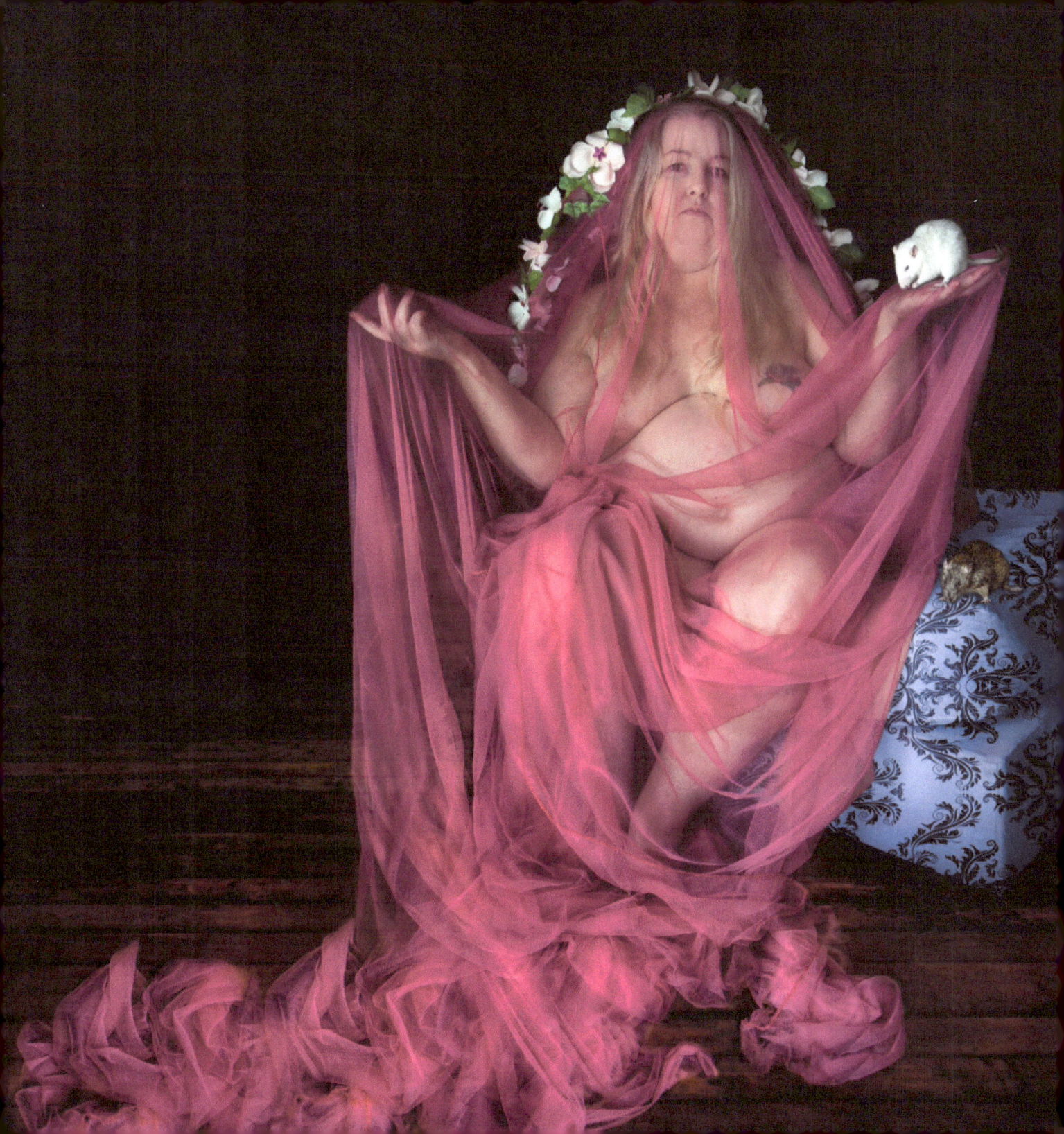

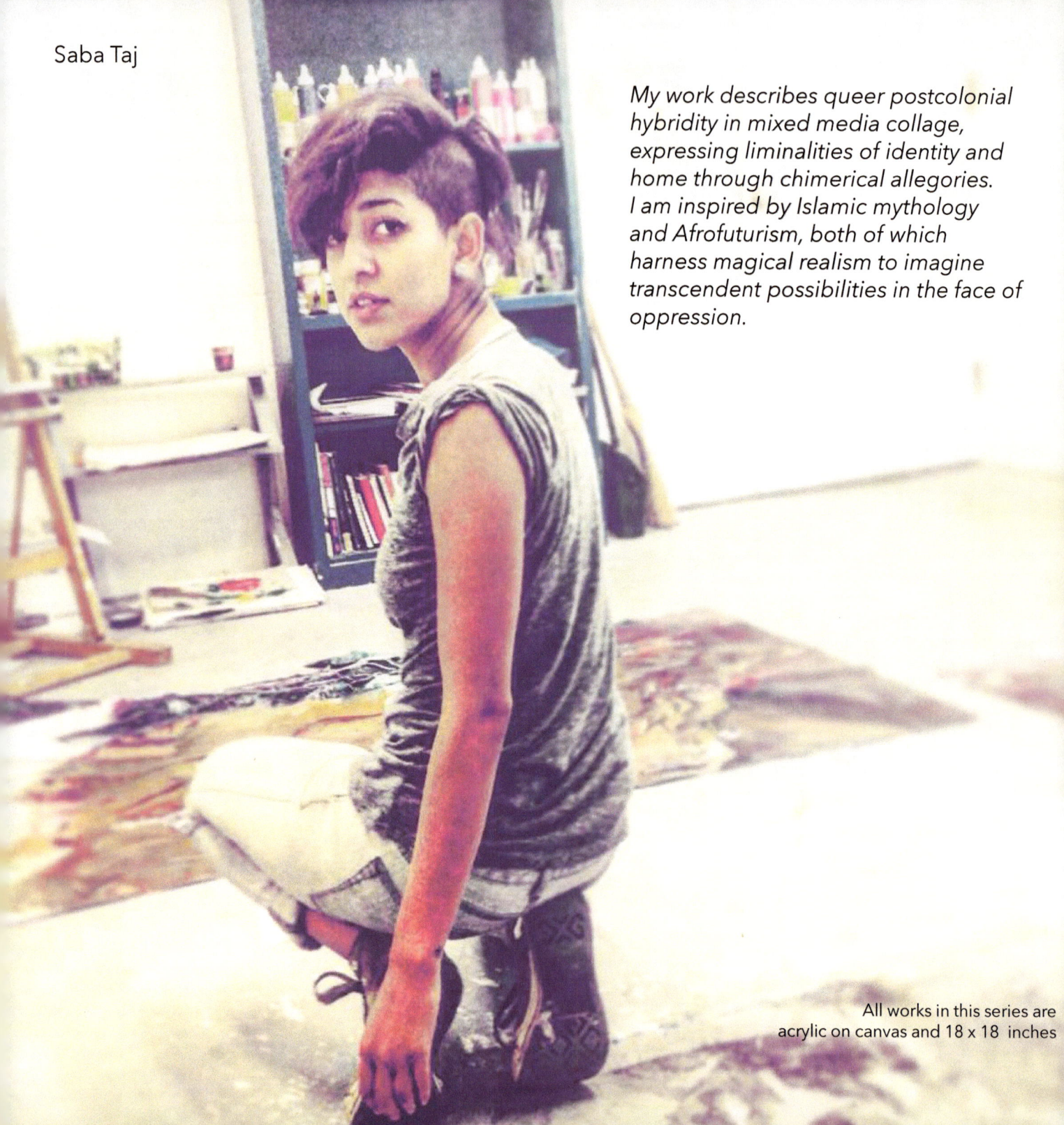

Saba Taj

My work describes queer postcolonial hybridity in mixed media collage, expressing liminalities of identity and home through chimerical allegories. I am inspired by Islamic mythology and Afrofuturism, both of which harness magical realism to imagine transcendent possibilities in the face of oppression.

All works in this series are acrylic on canvas and 18 x 18 inches

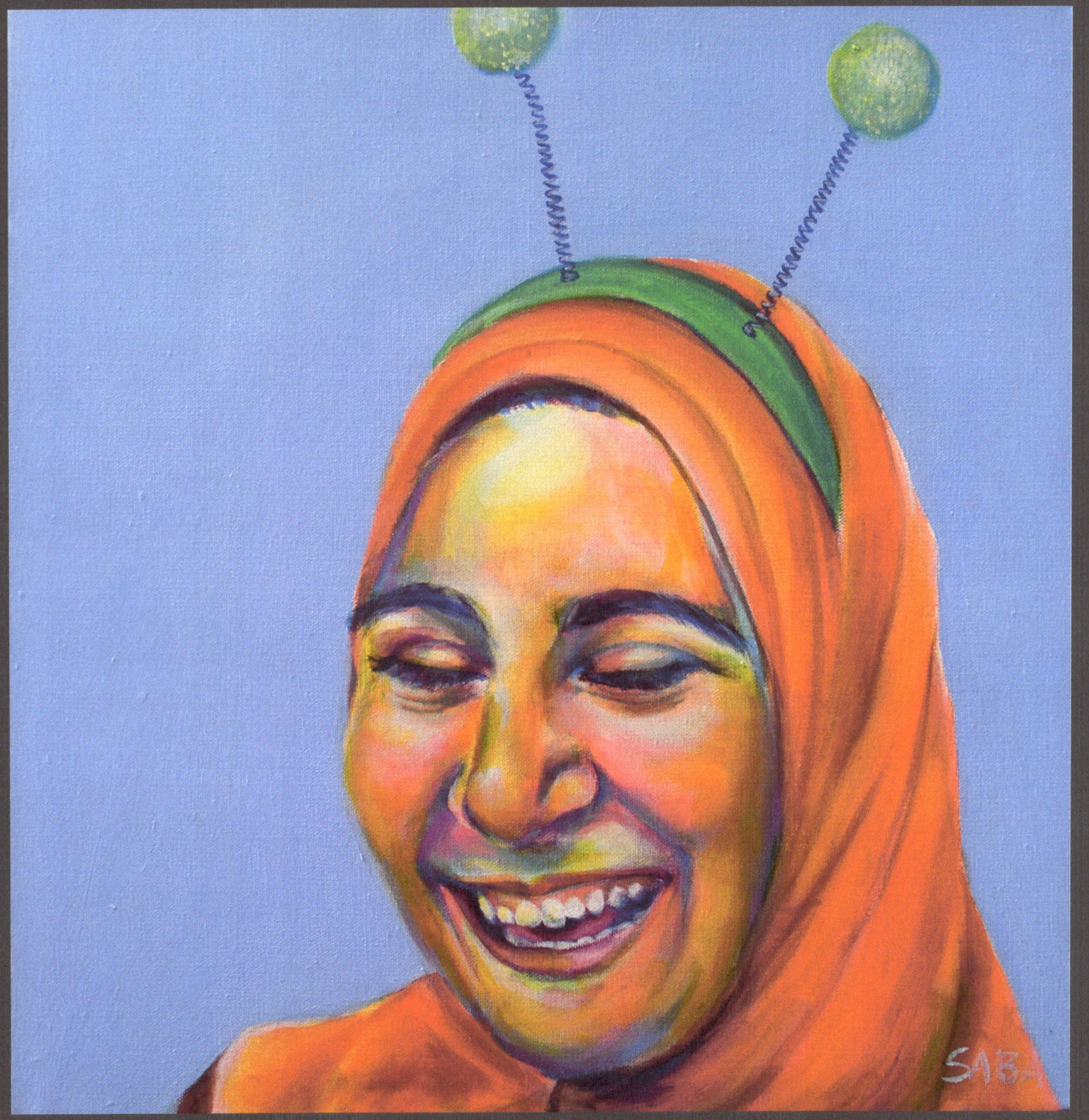

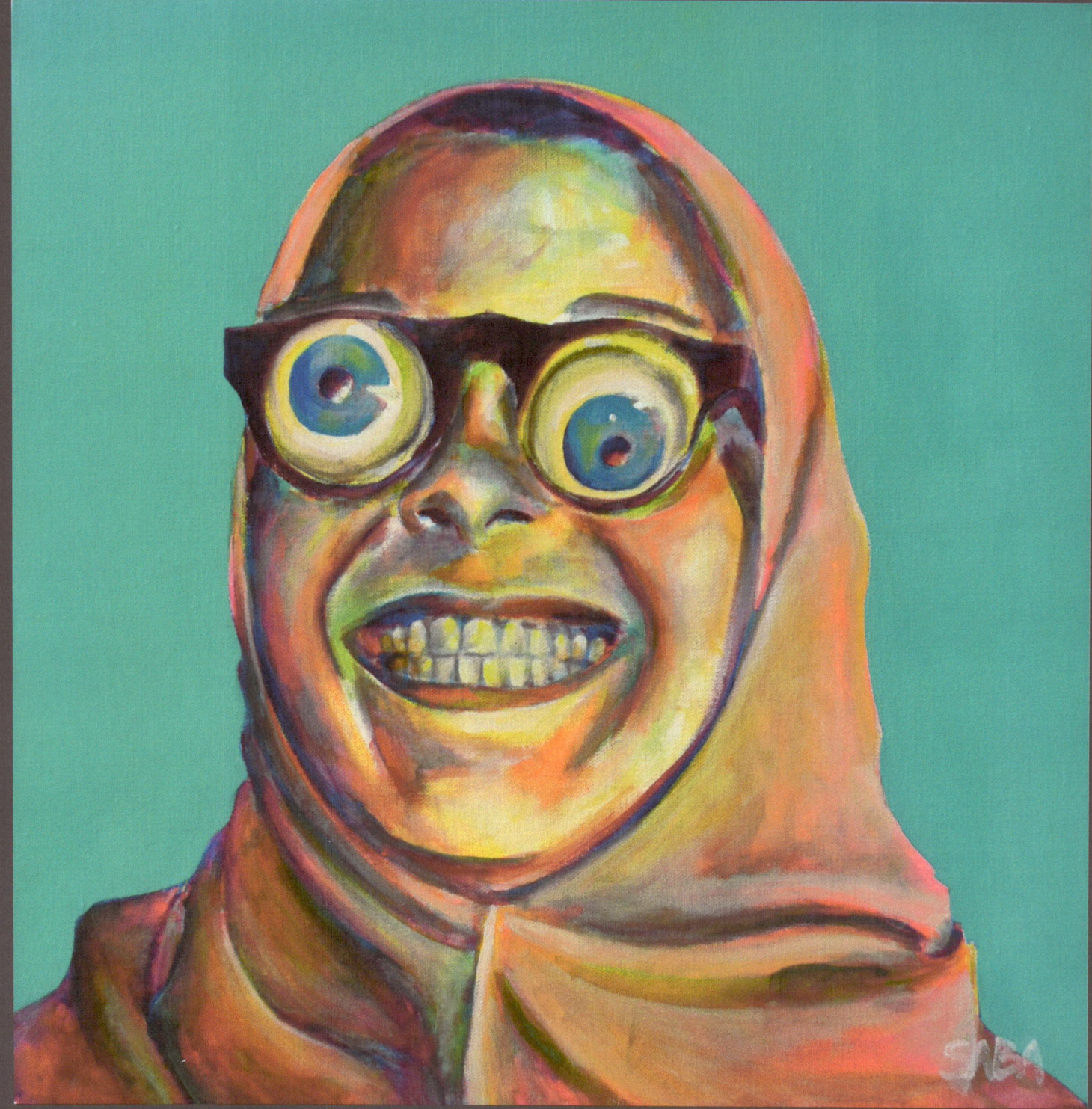

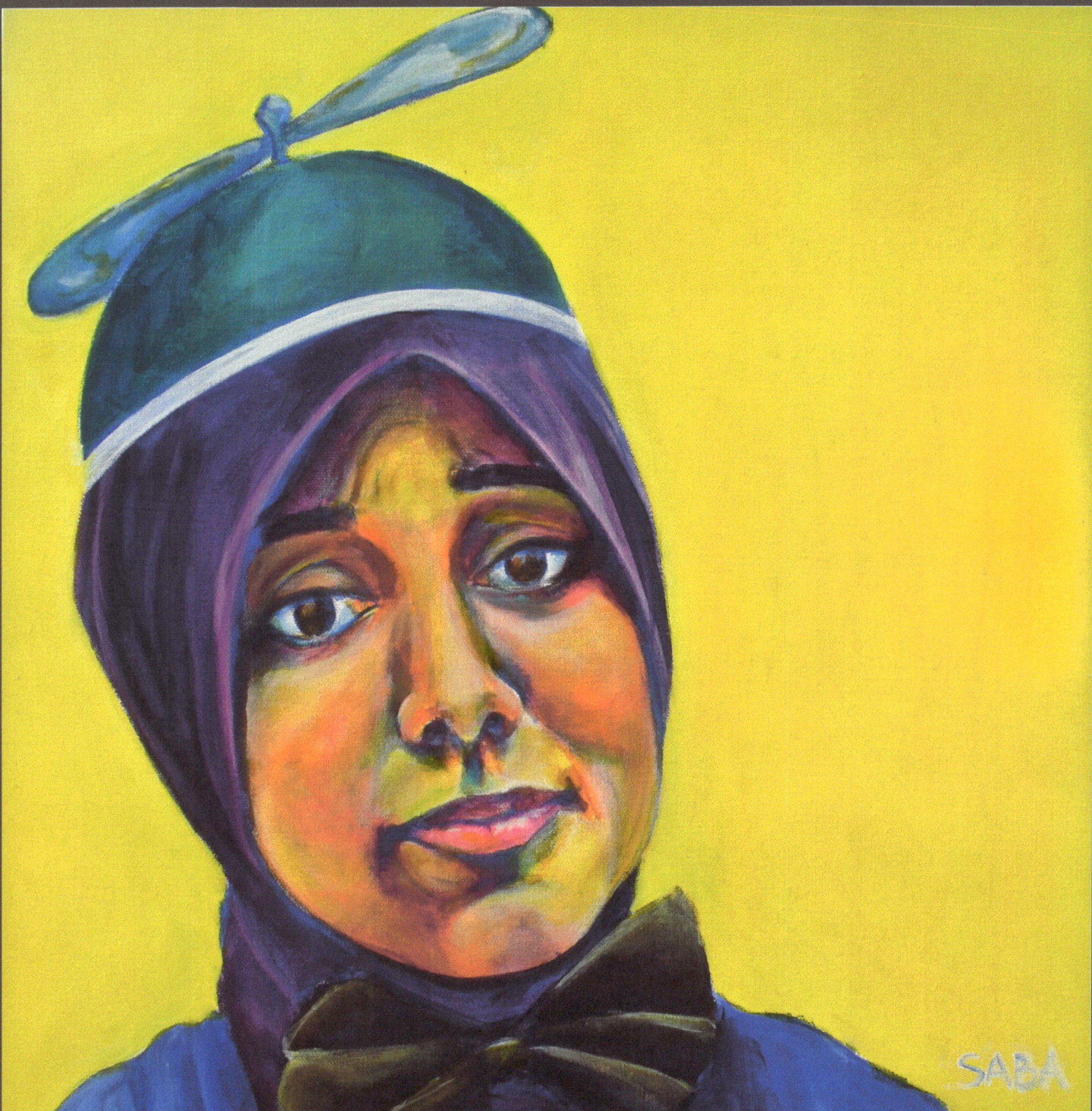

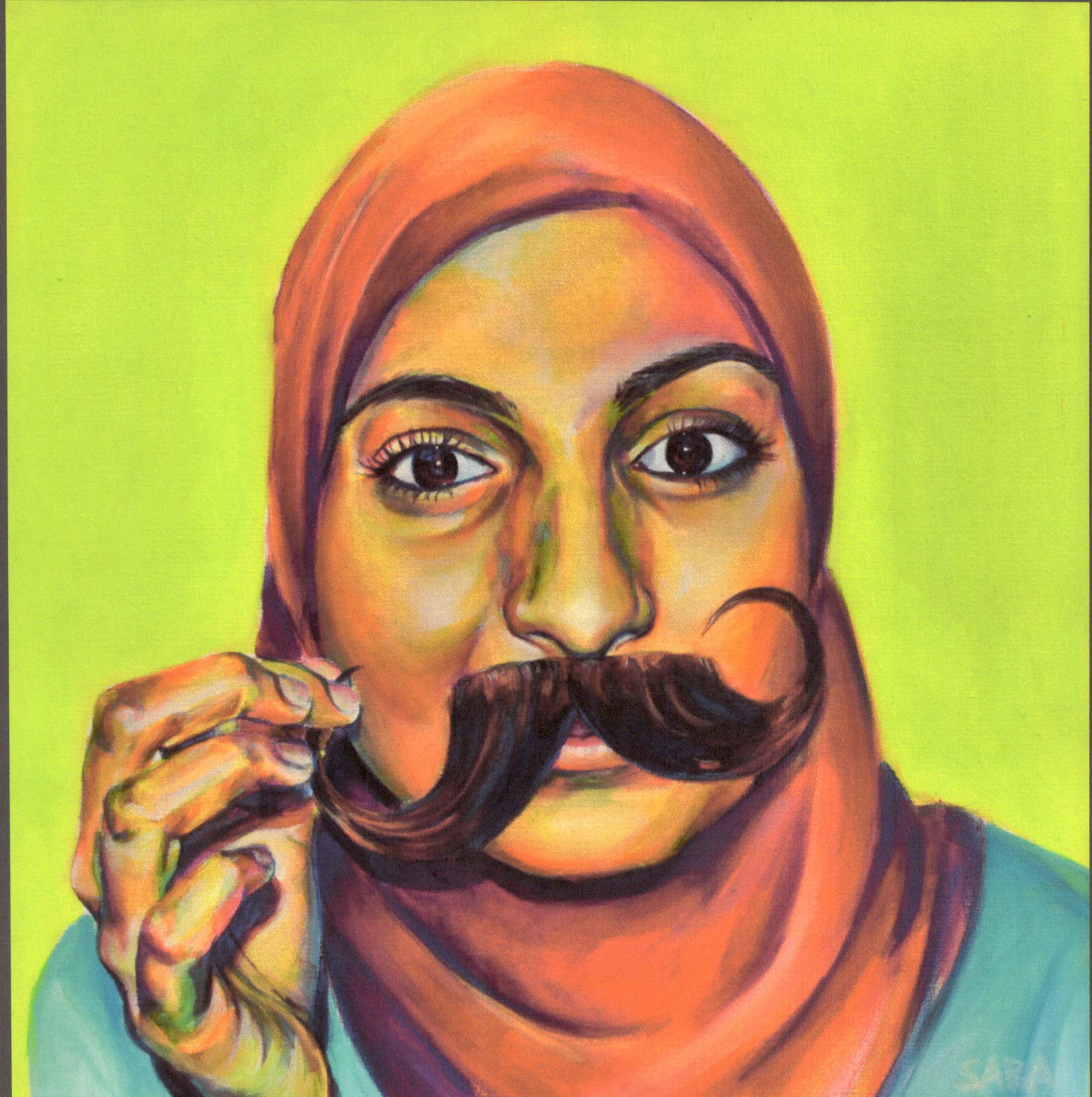

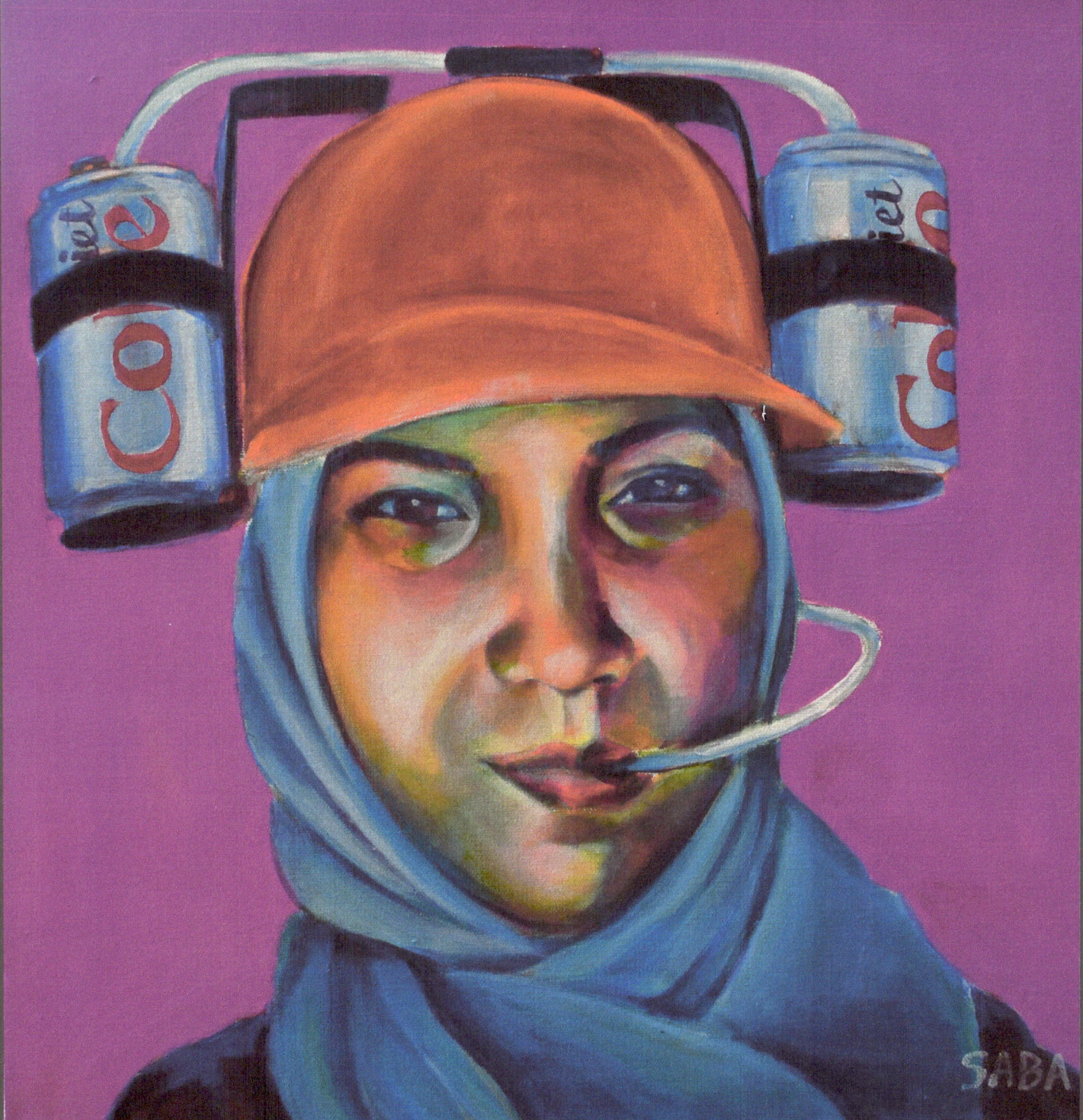

Guanyu Xu

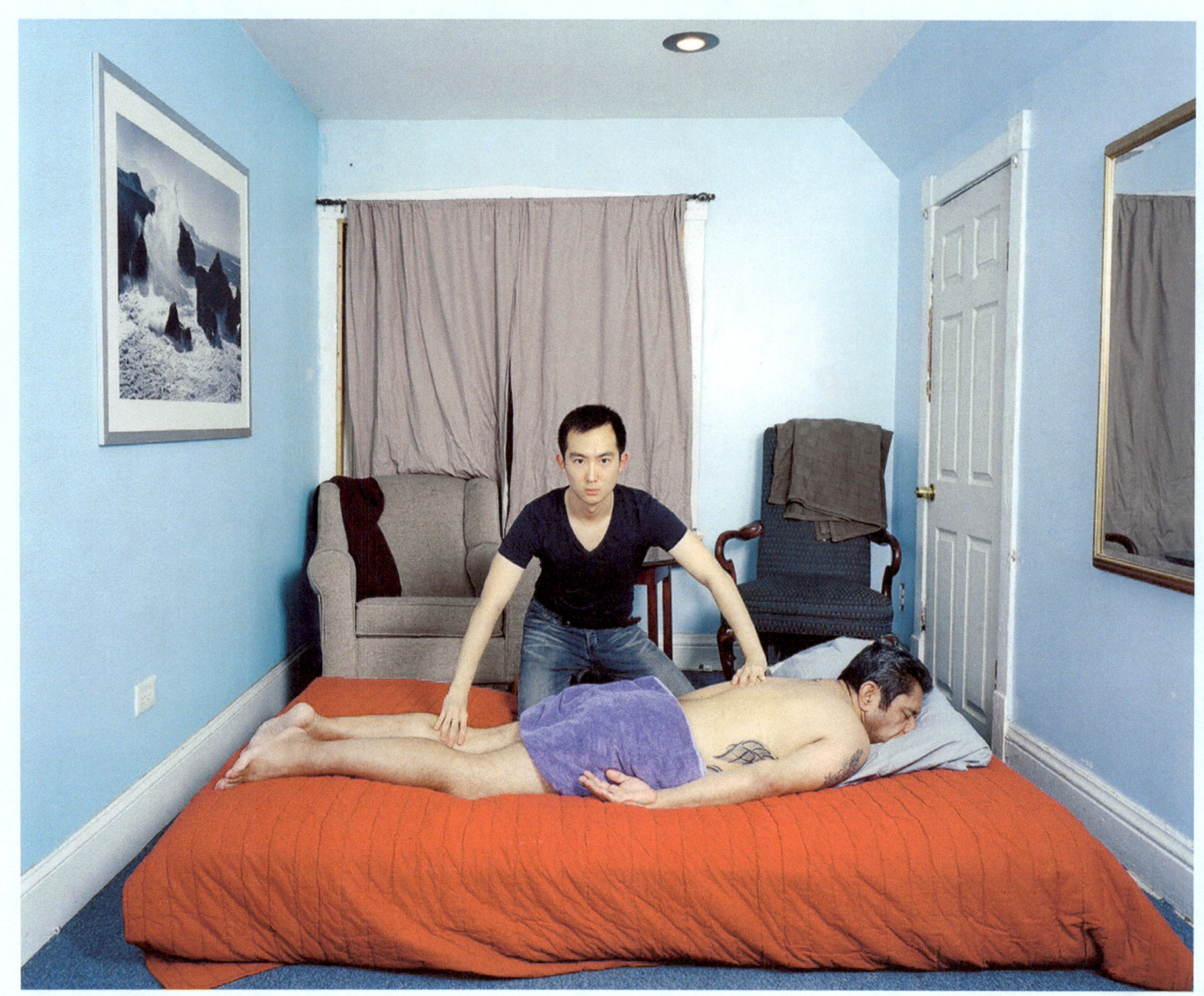

Blind Massage | photography prints | 16 x 20 inches

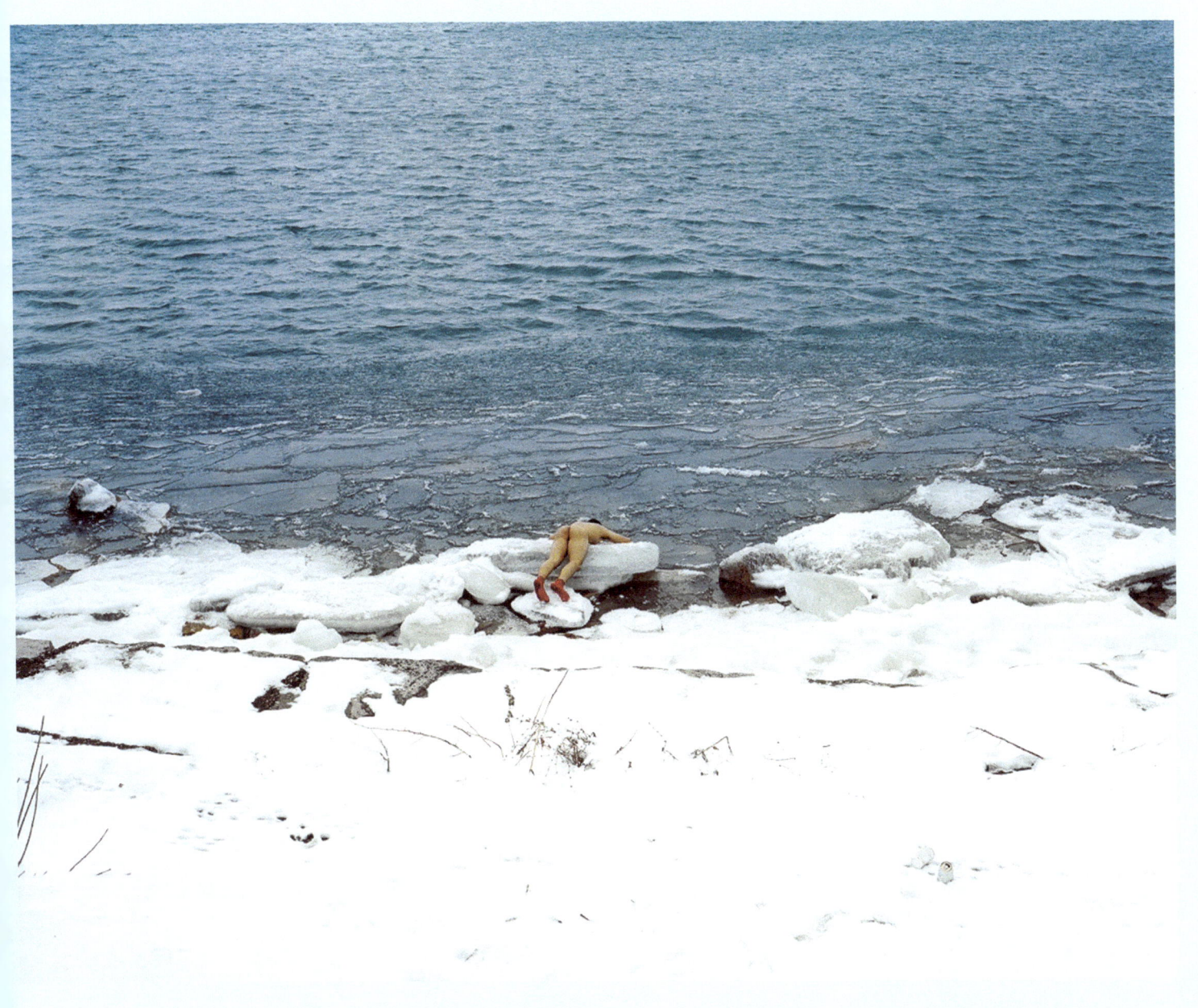

Sea (Lake Michigan) | photography prints | 16 x 20 inches

Lee Bullitt

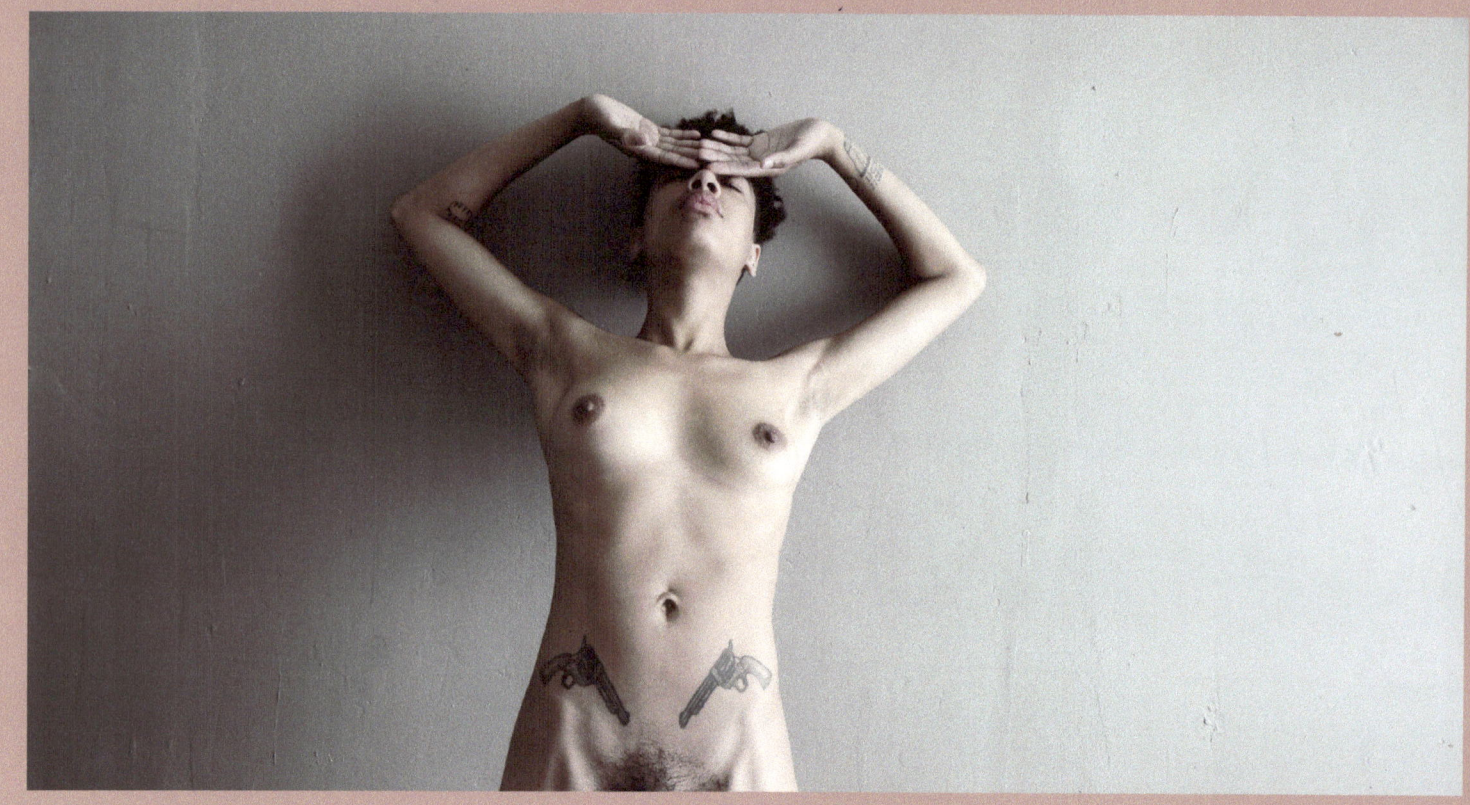

Fictitious External | Prints on Kodak Endura Luster Paper | 30 x 30 inches

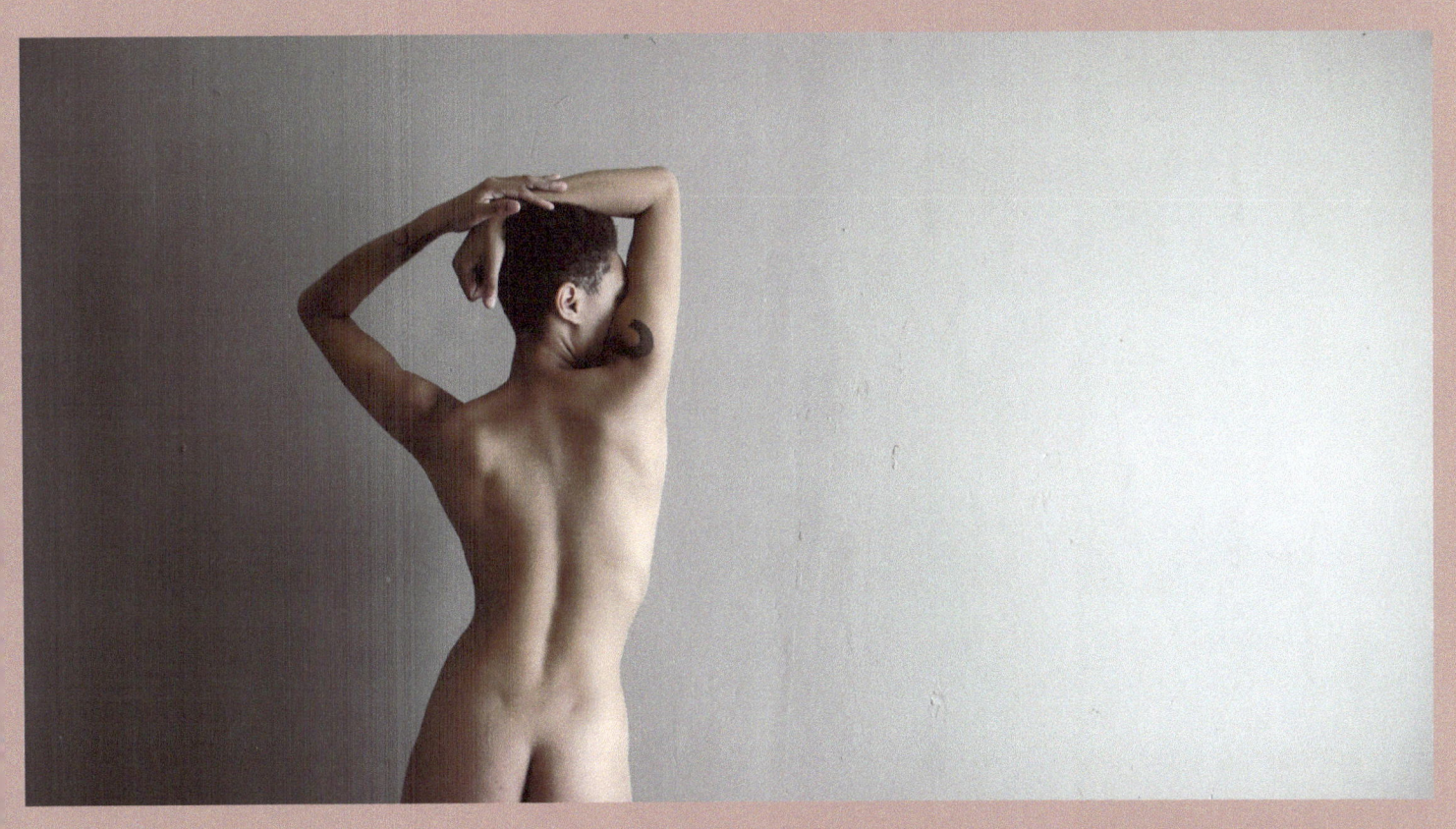

Internal Processing | Prints on Kodak Endura Luster Paper | 30 x 30 inches

Daniel Gamez

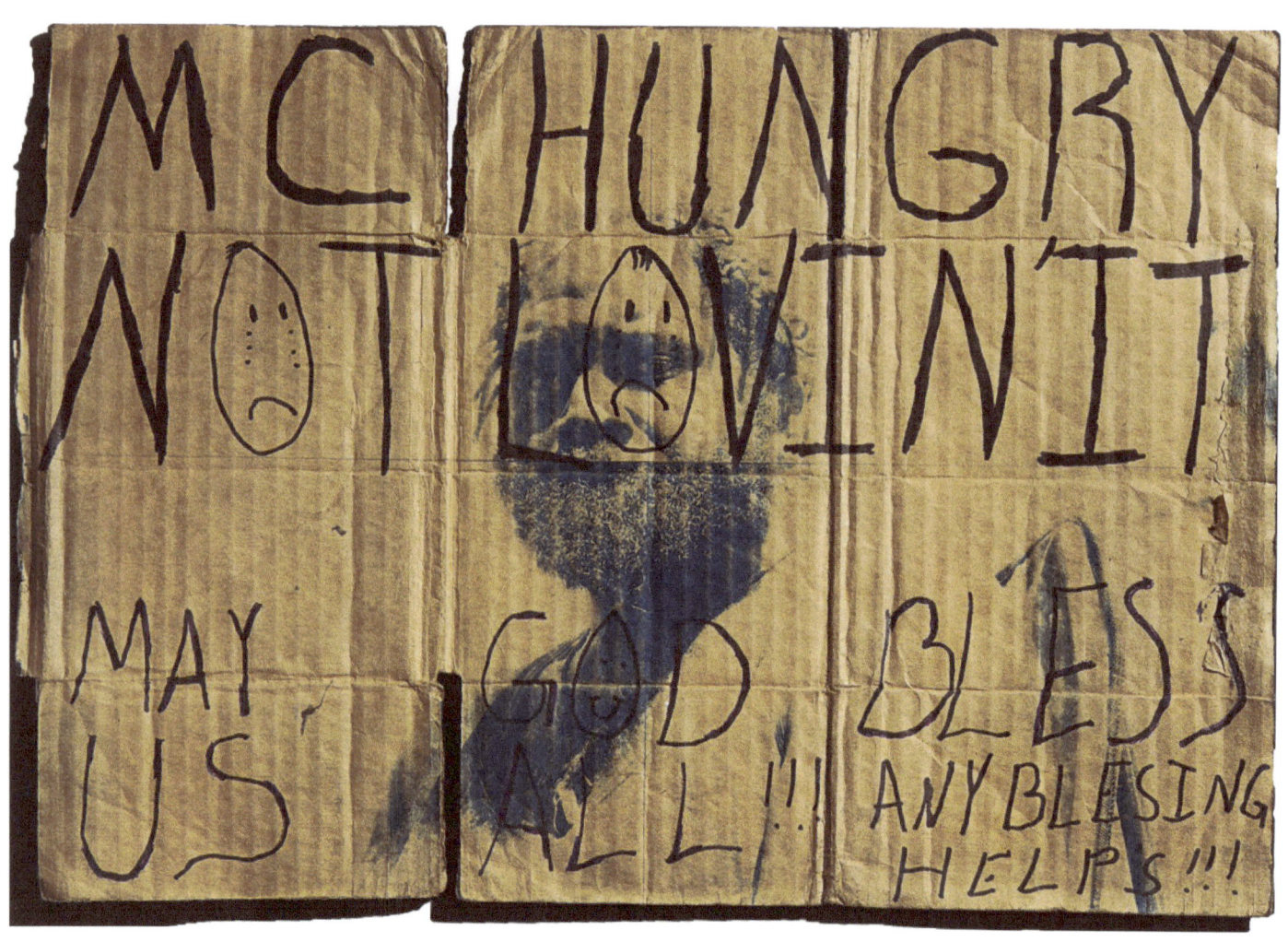

Dyon Johnson, MC HUNGRY

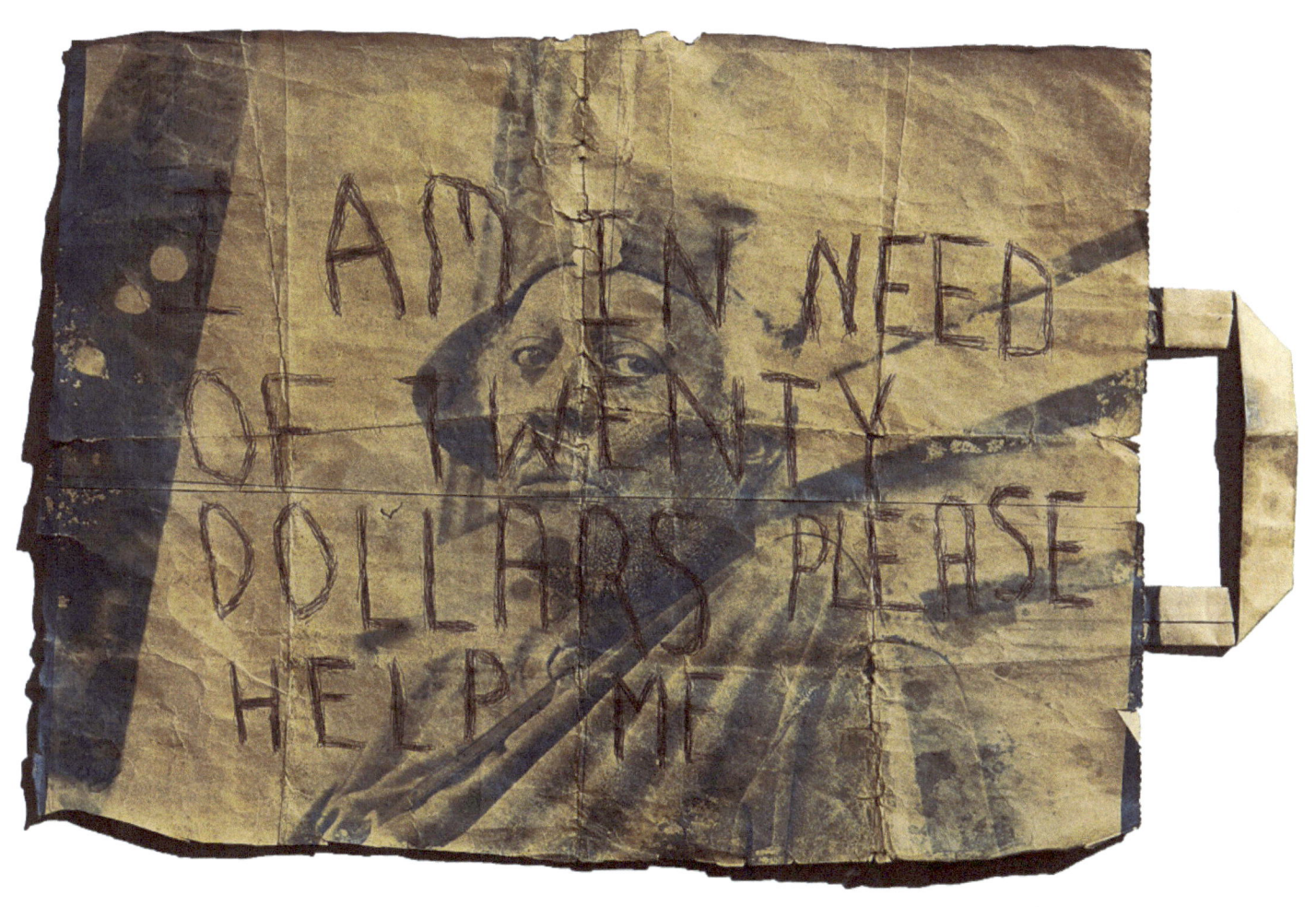

Steven Lewis, I AM IN NEED

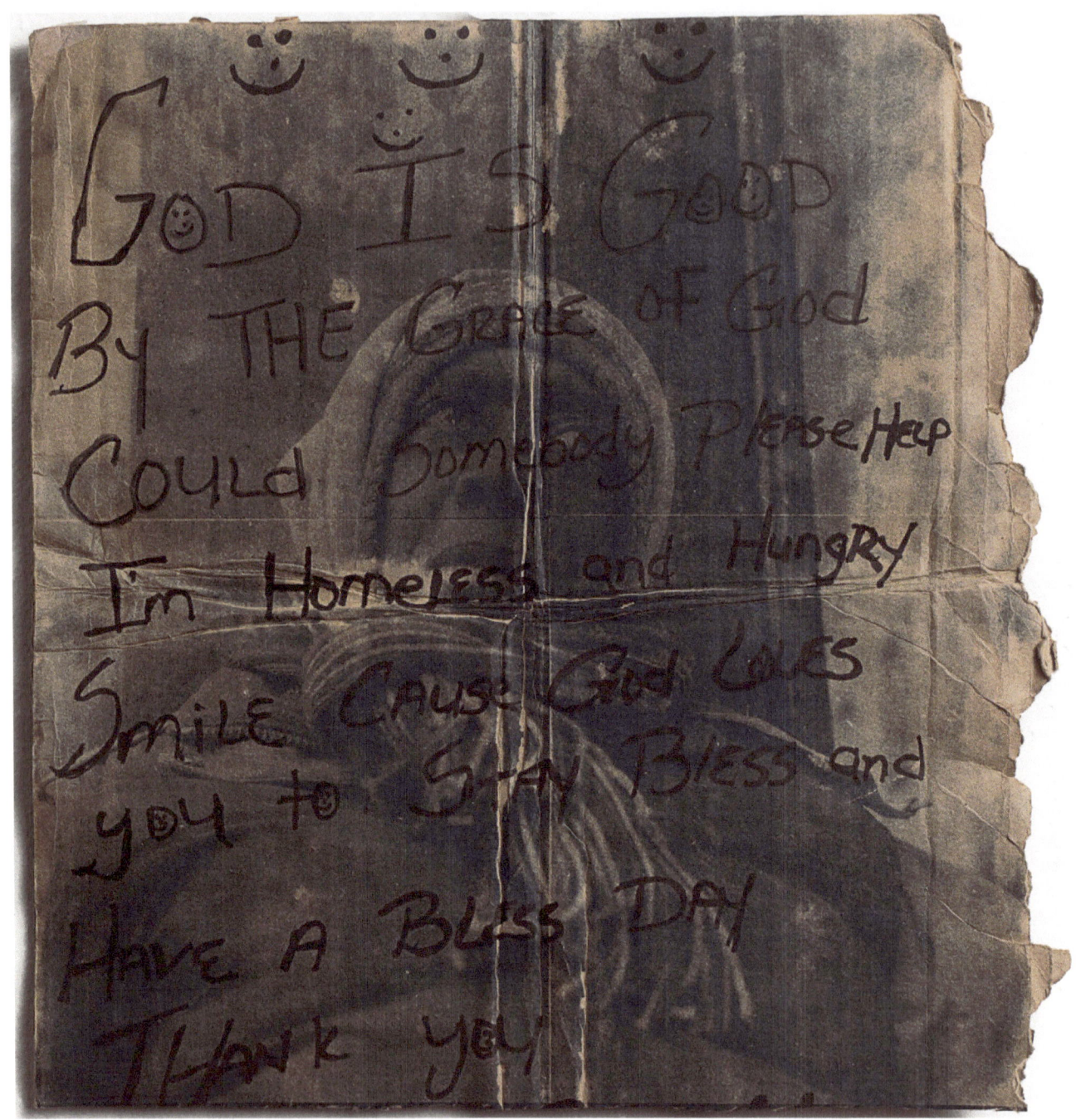

Brenda Jackson, GOD IS GOOD

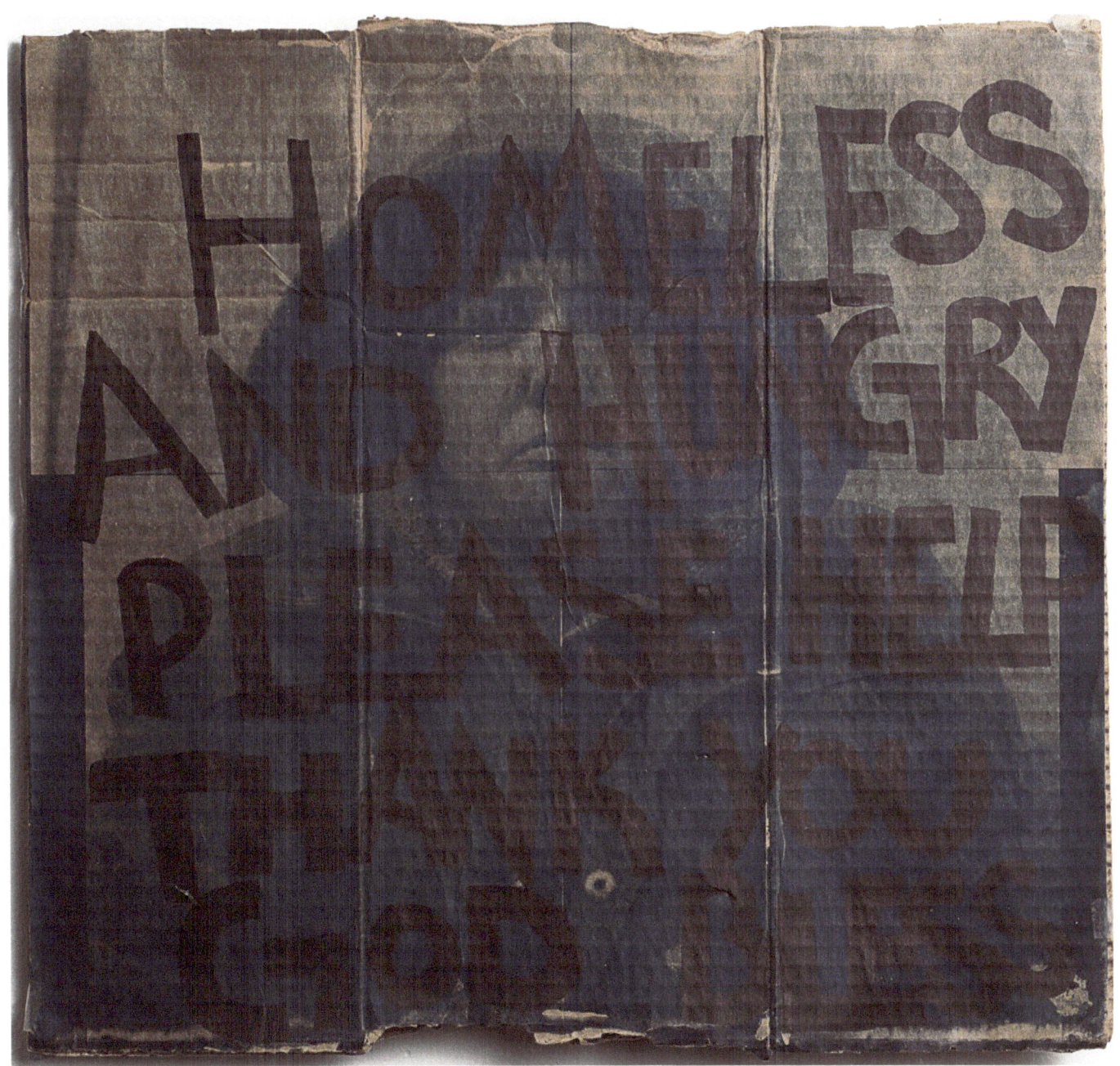

Tracie Pinker, HOMELESS AND HUNGRY

Reisha

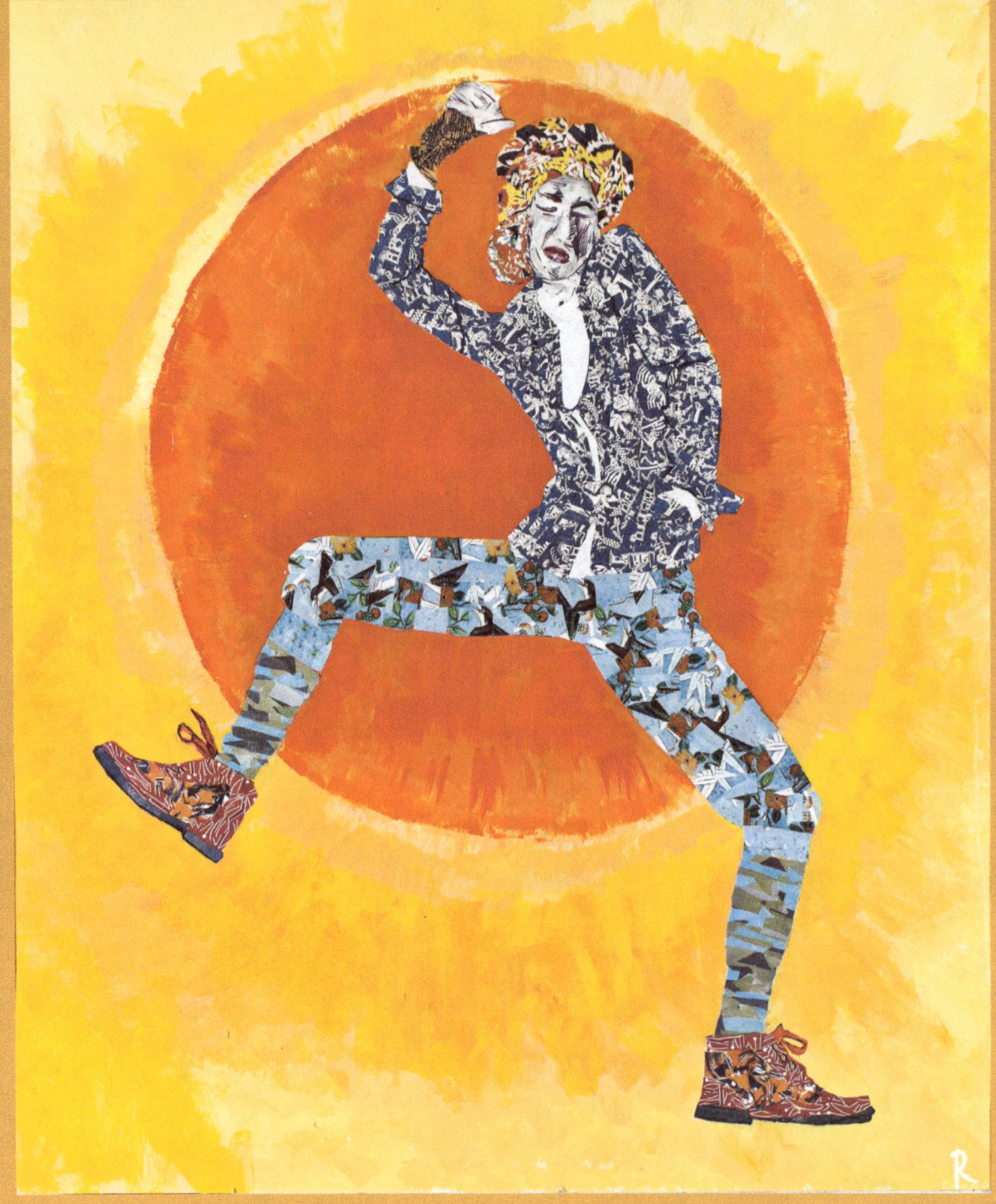

Lady Del Sol | mixed media collage on wood | 41 x 48 inches

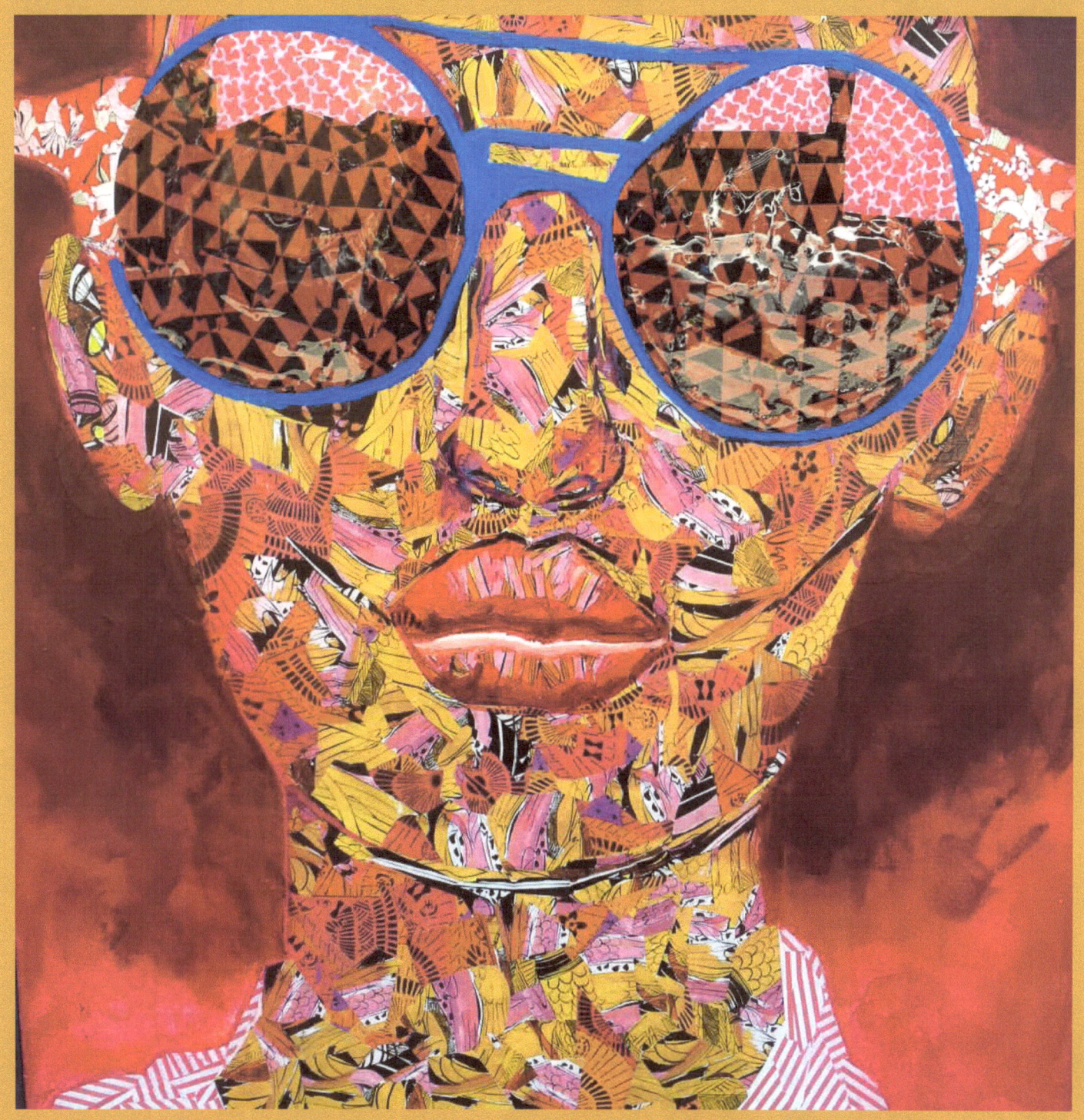

Jon/Joan Jenner | mixed media collage on canvas | 20 x 20 inches

Victoria Selbach

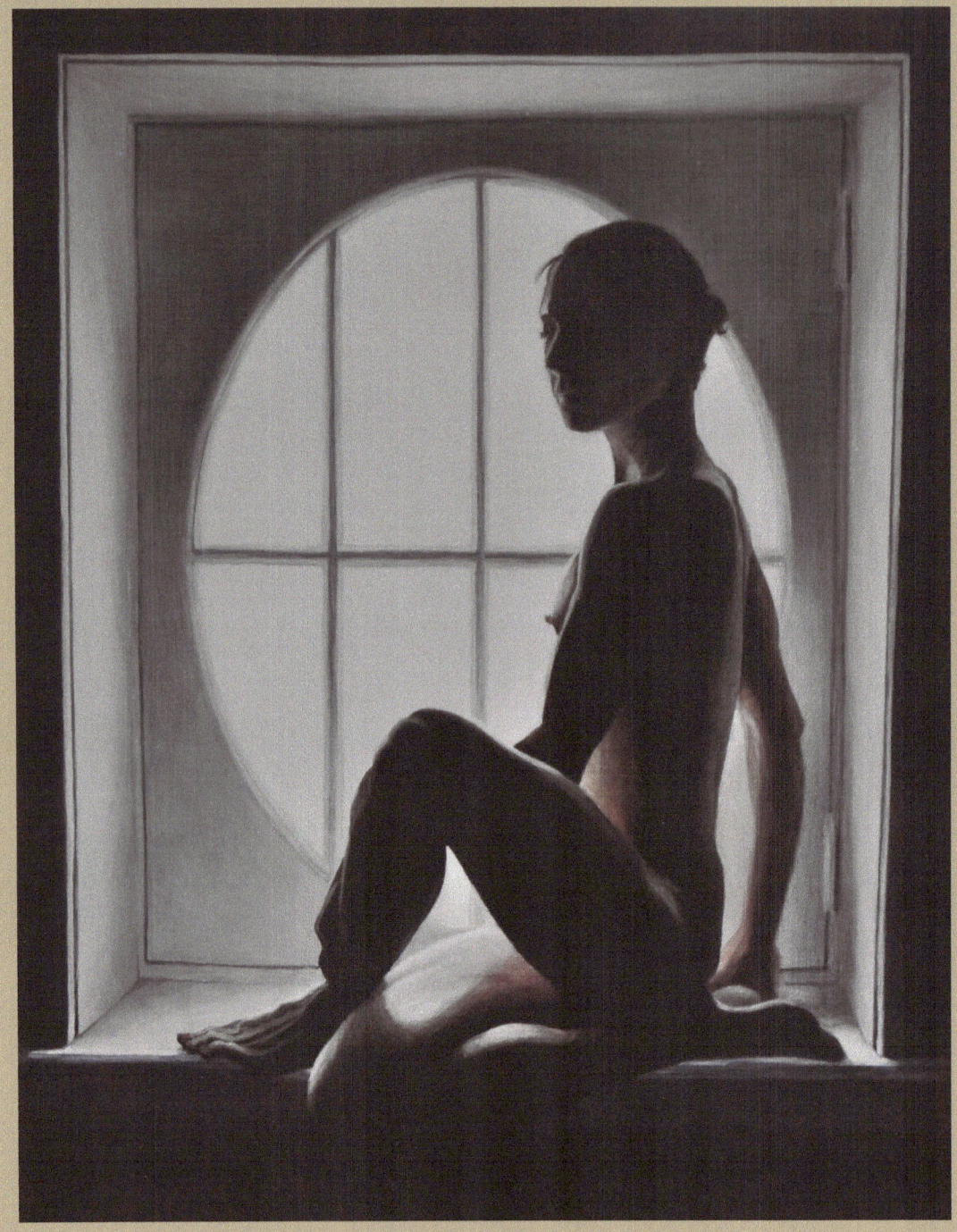

Earthly | acrylic on wood panel | 20 x 16 inches

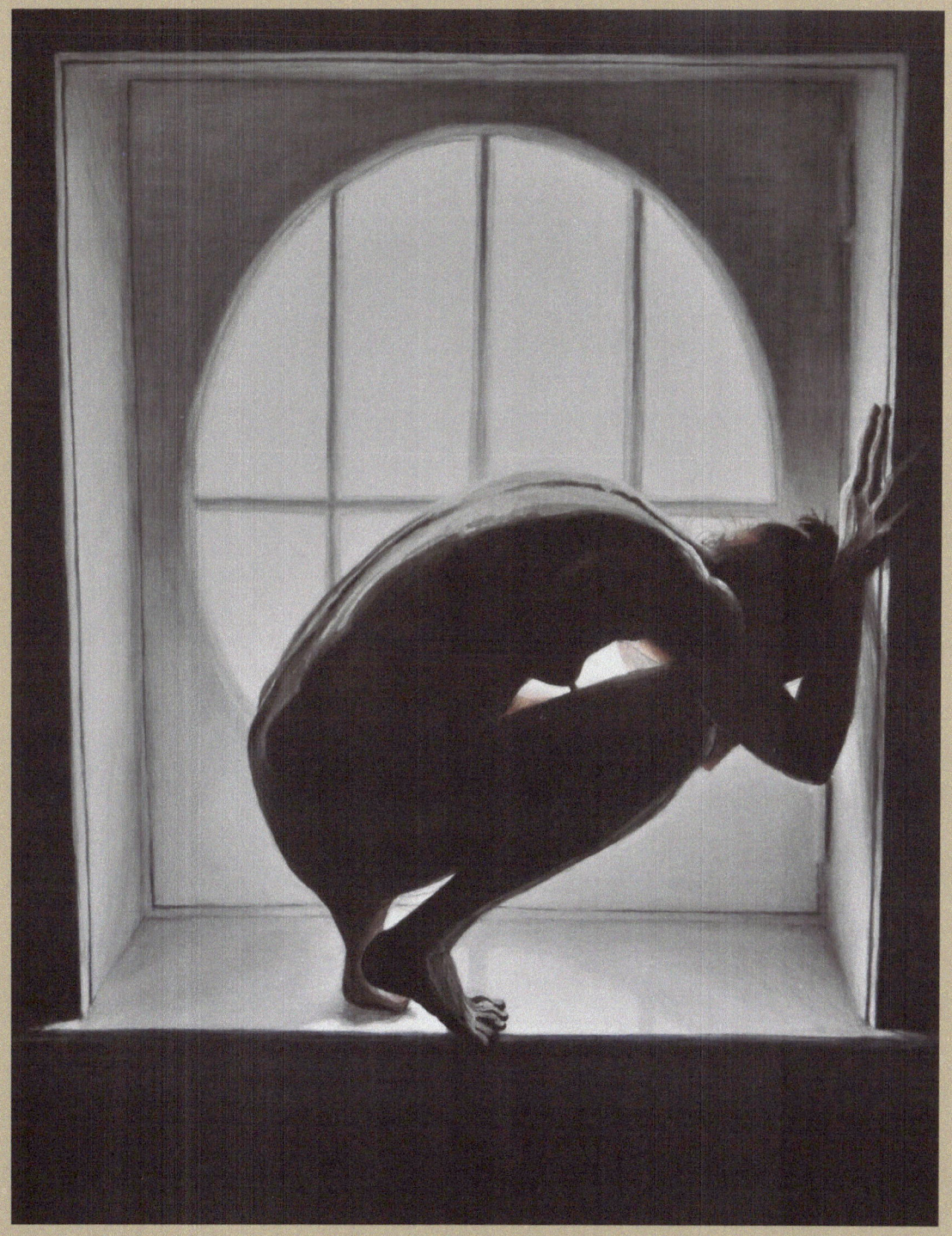

Saintly | acrylic on wood panel | 20 x 16 inches

Myia N. Brown

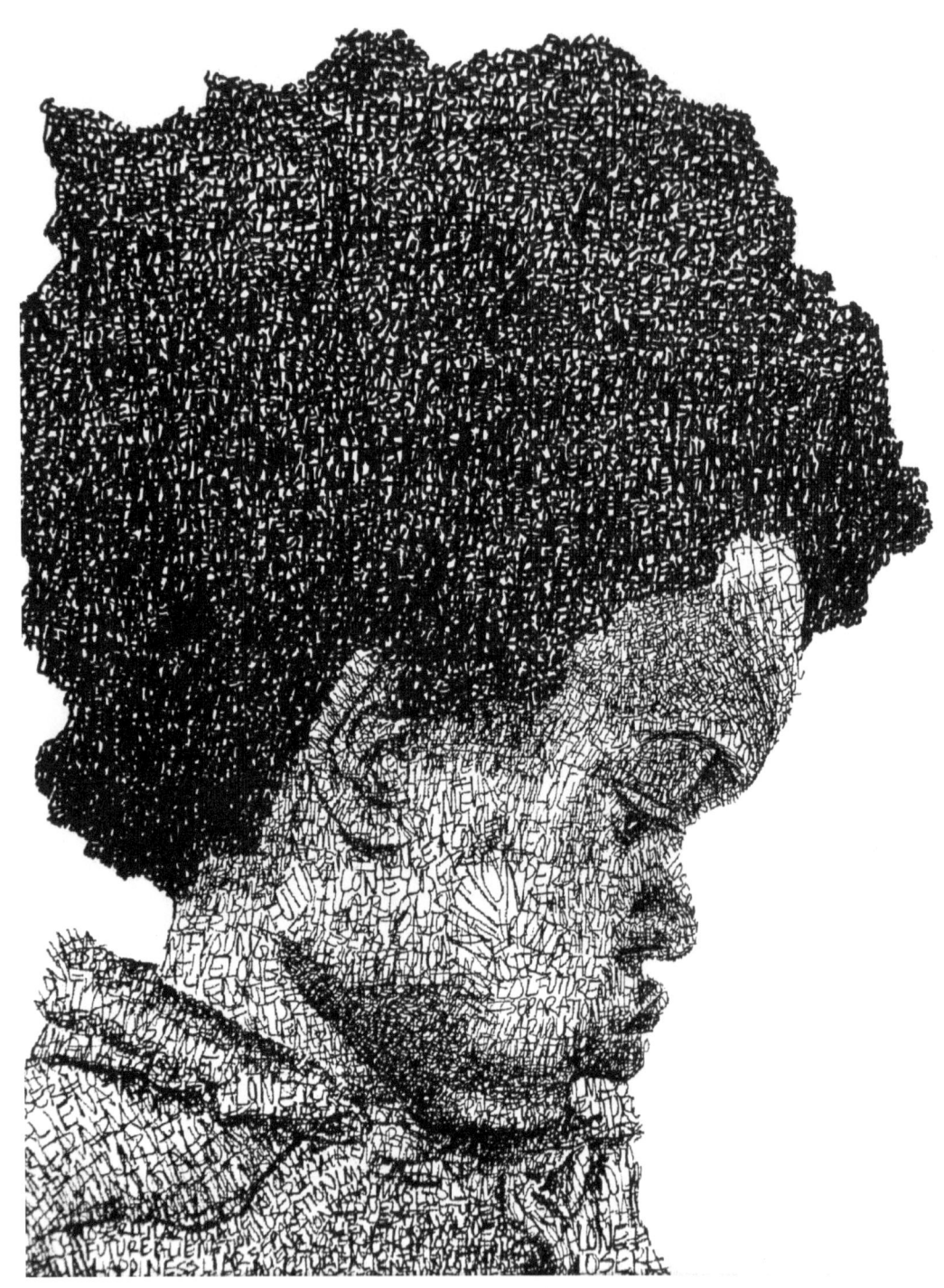

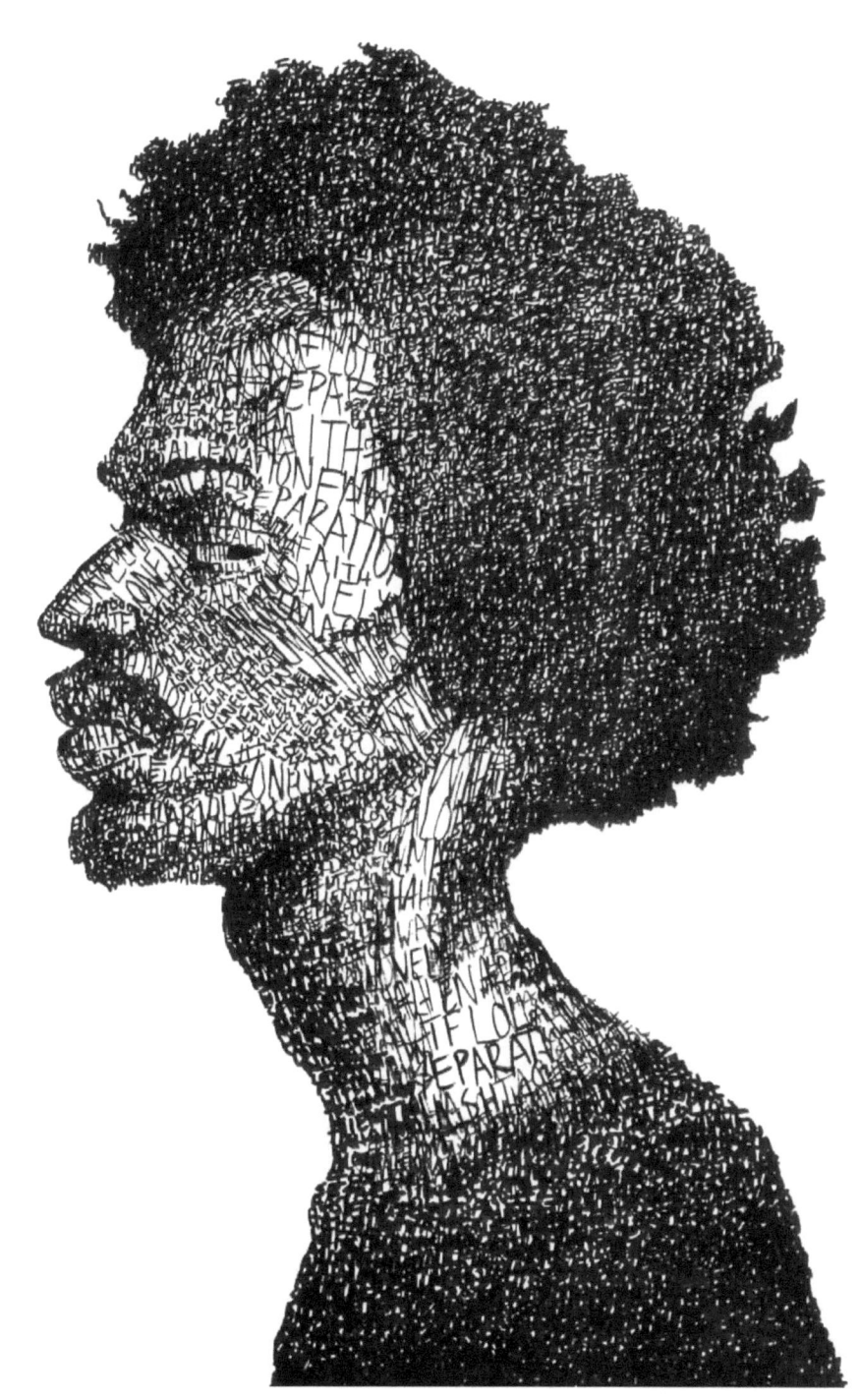

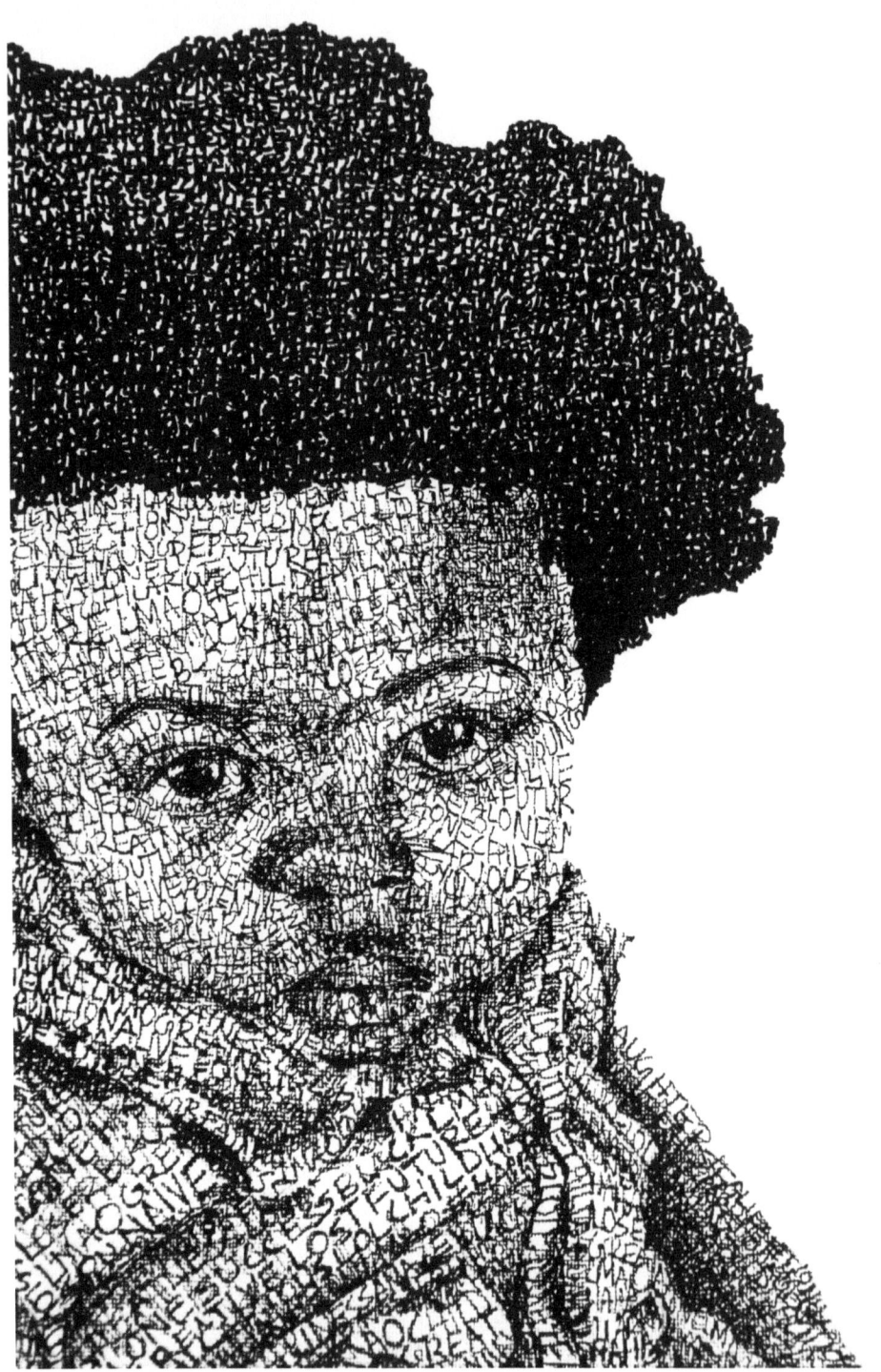

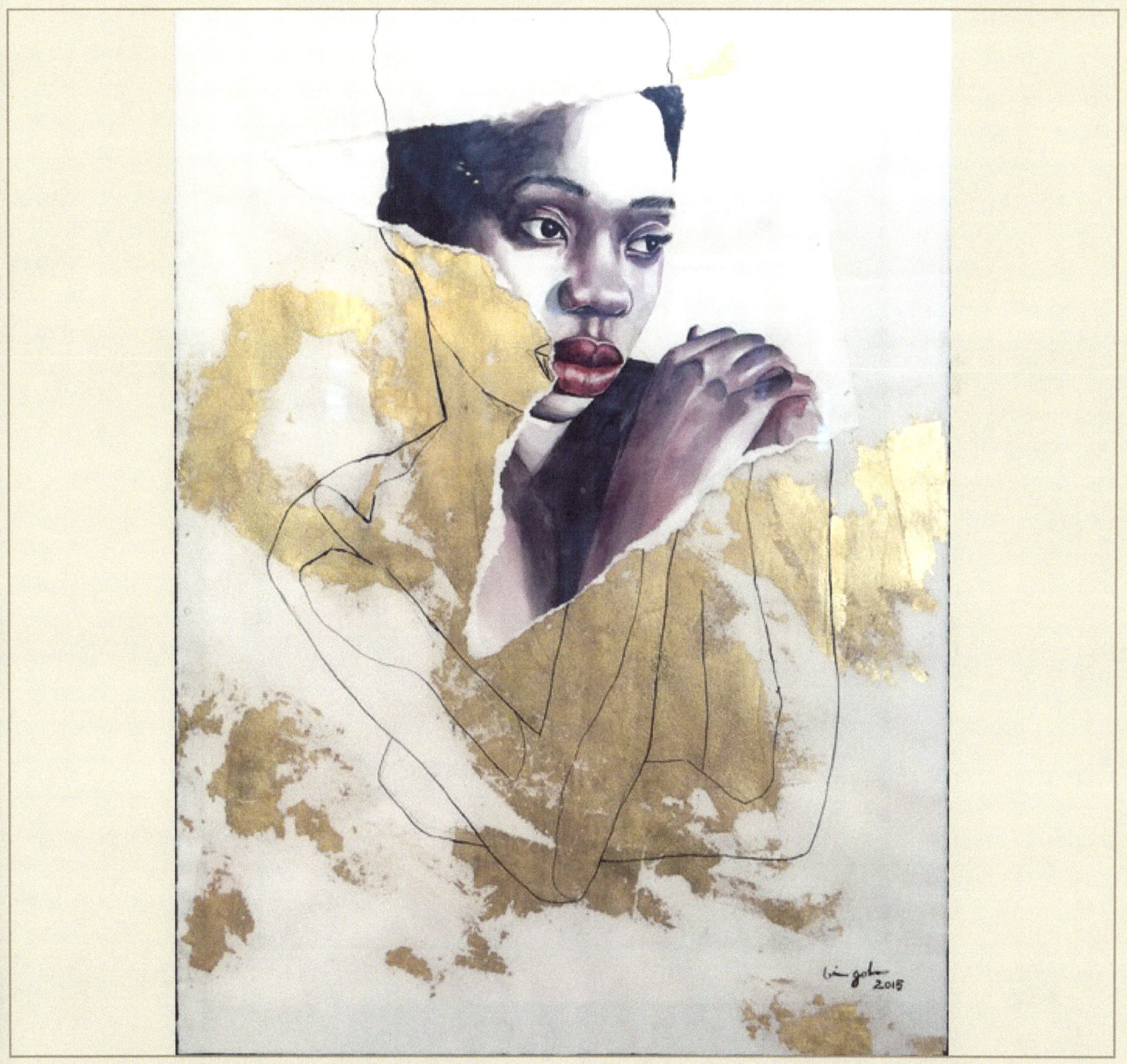

Balancing Act | Watercolor, Ink, and Gold Leaf on Paper

David Anthony Geary

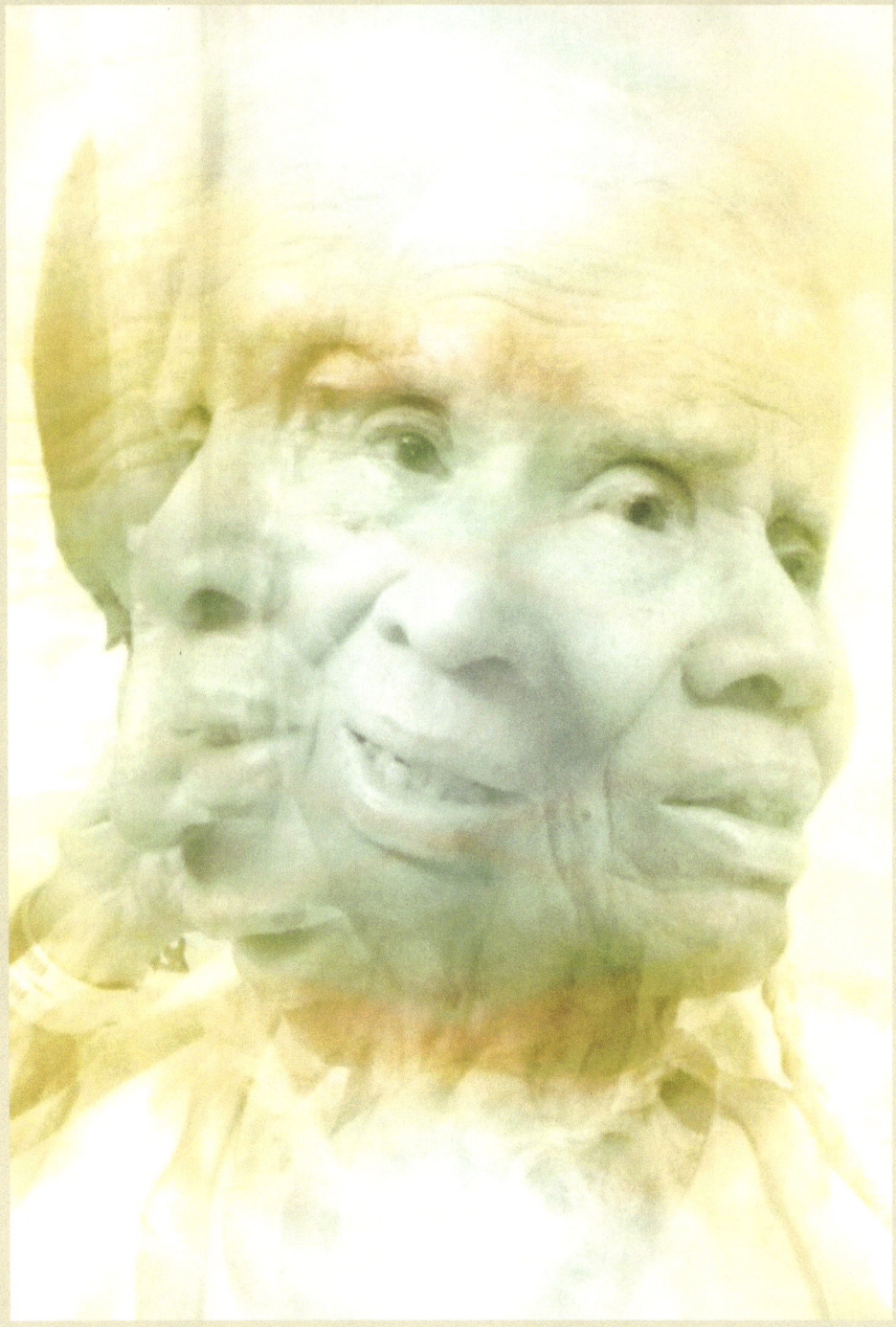

Our Last Conversation | photography and mixed media | 20 x 30 inches

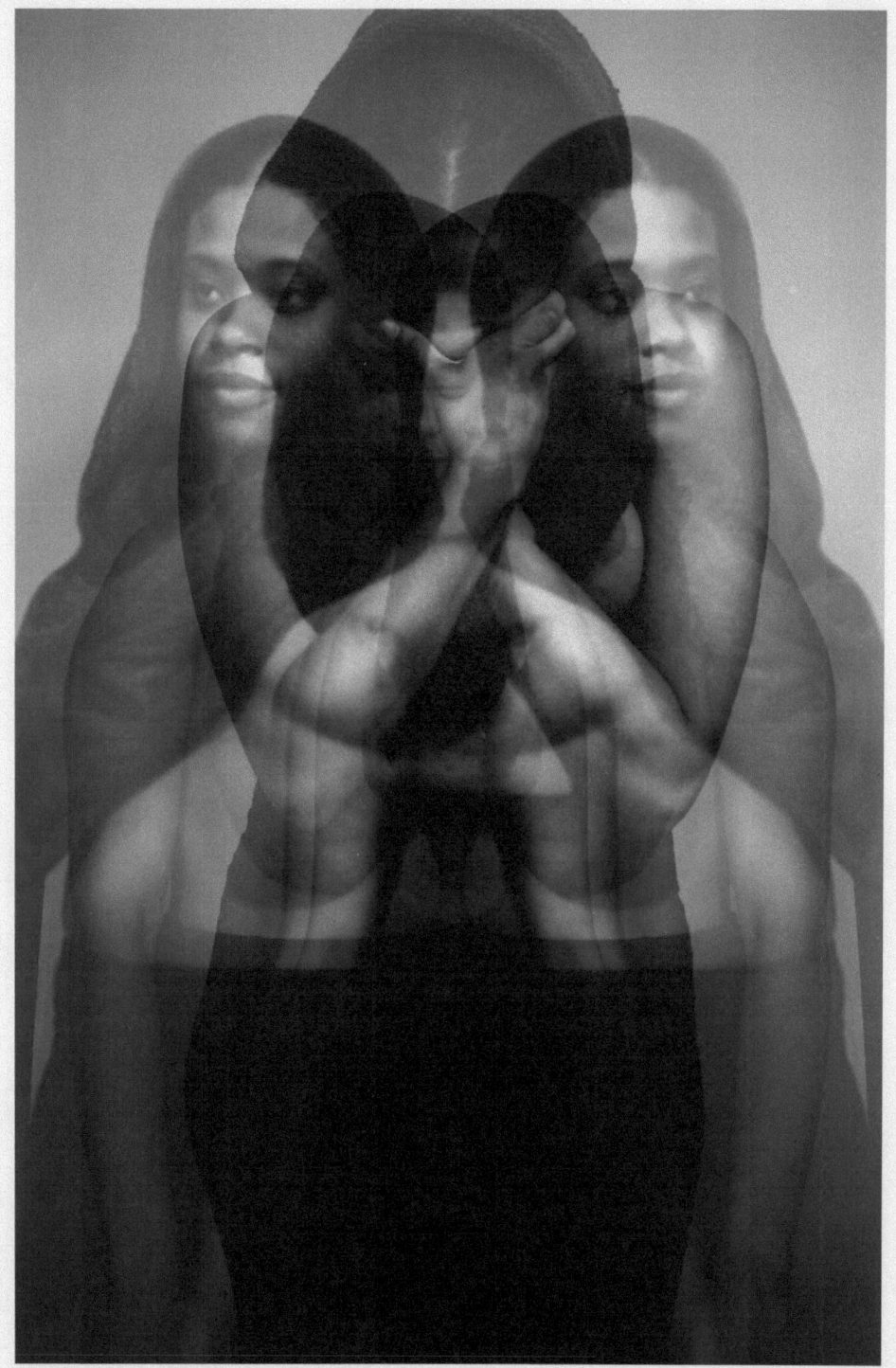

Intro/Extro | photography and mixed media | 20 x 30 inches

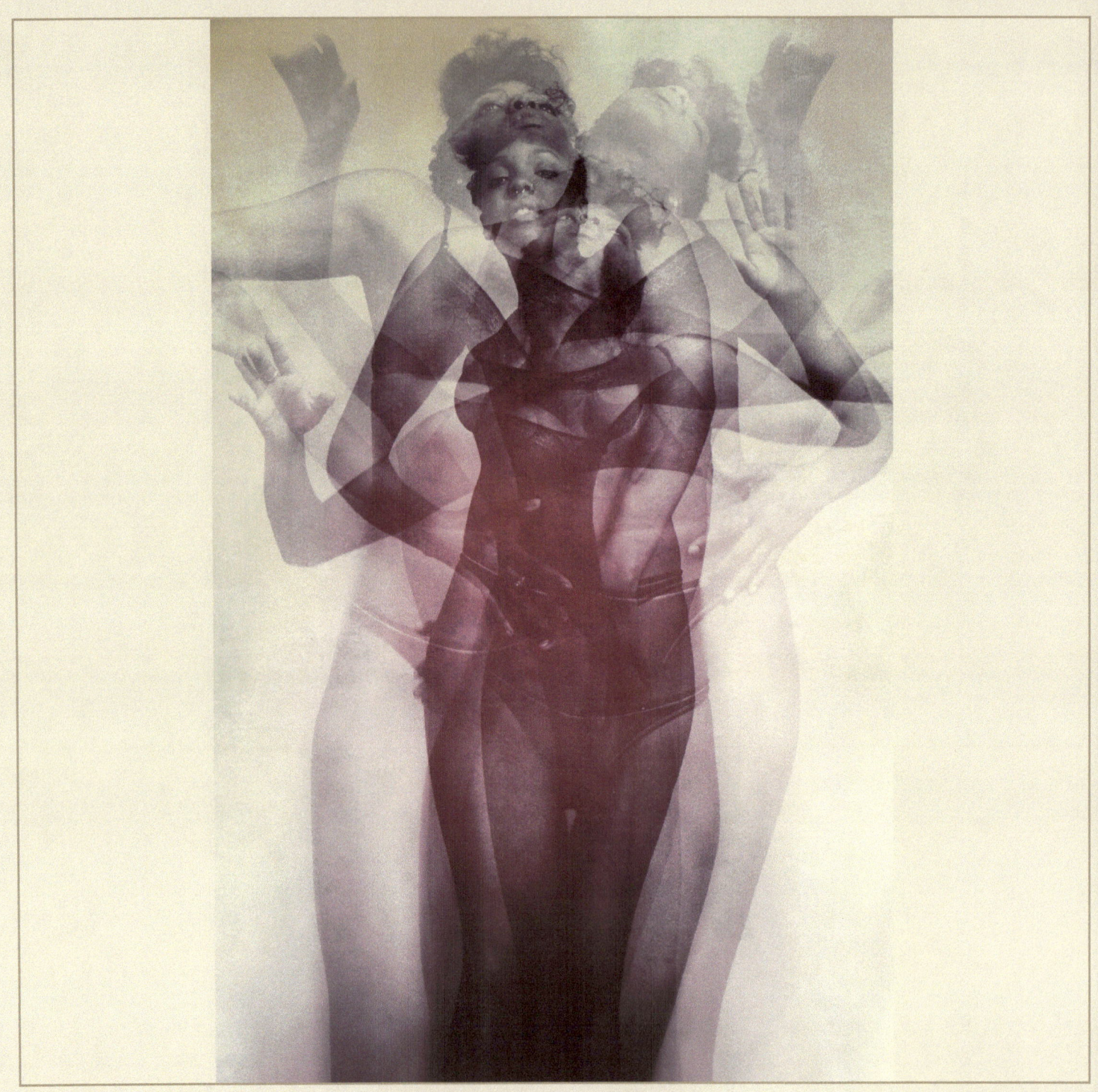

Release | photography and mixed media | 20 x 30 inches

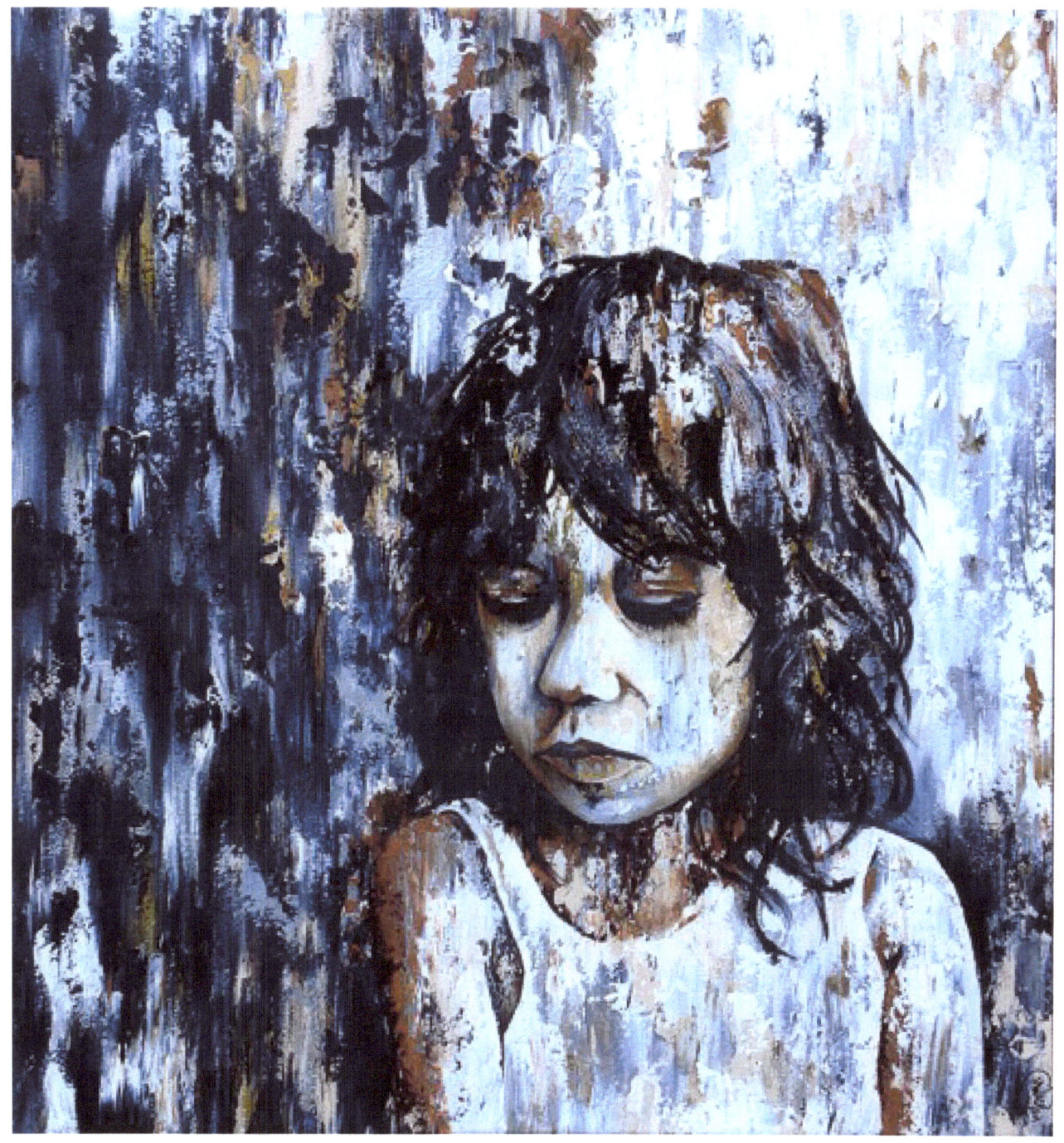

The Dreamer | acrylic on canvas | 36 x 38 inches

Brandon Breaux

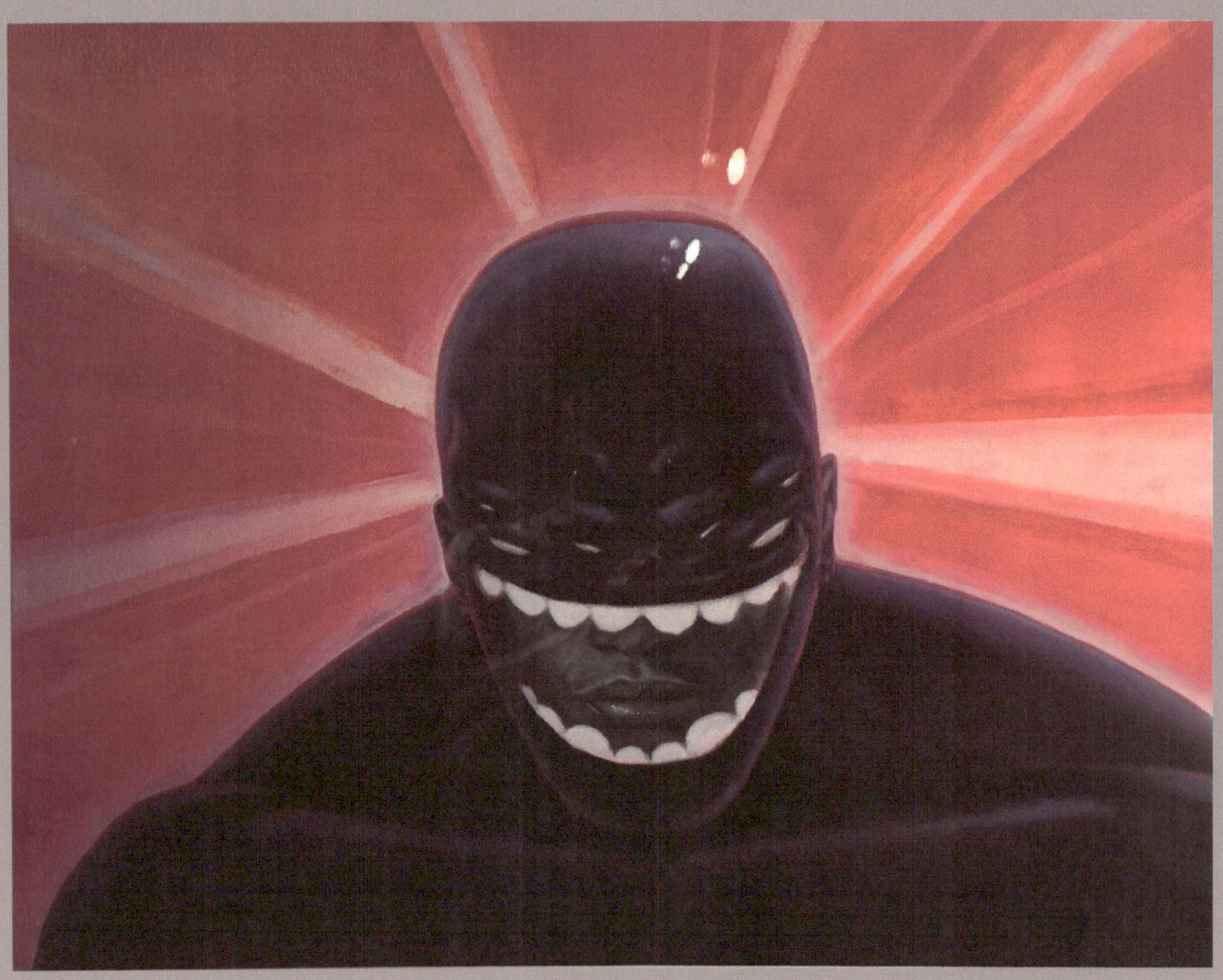

Within | oil on gesso paper | 27.5 x 22 inches

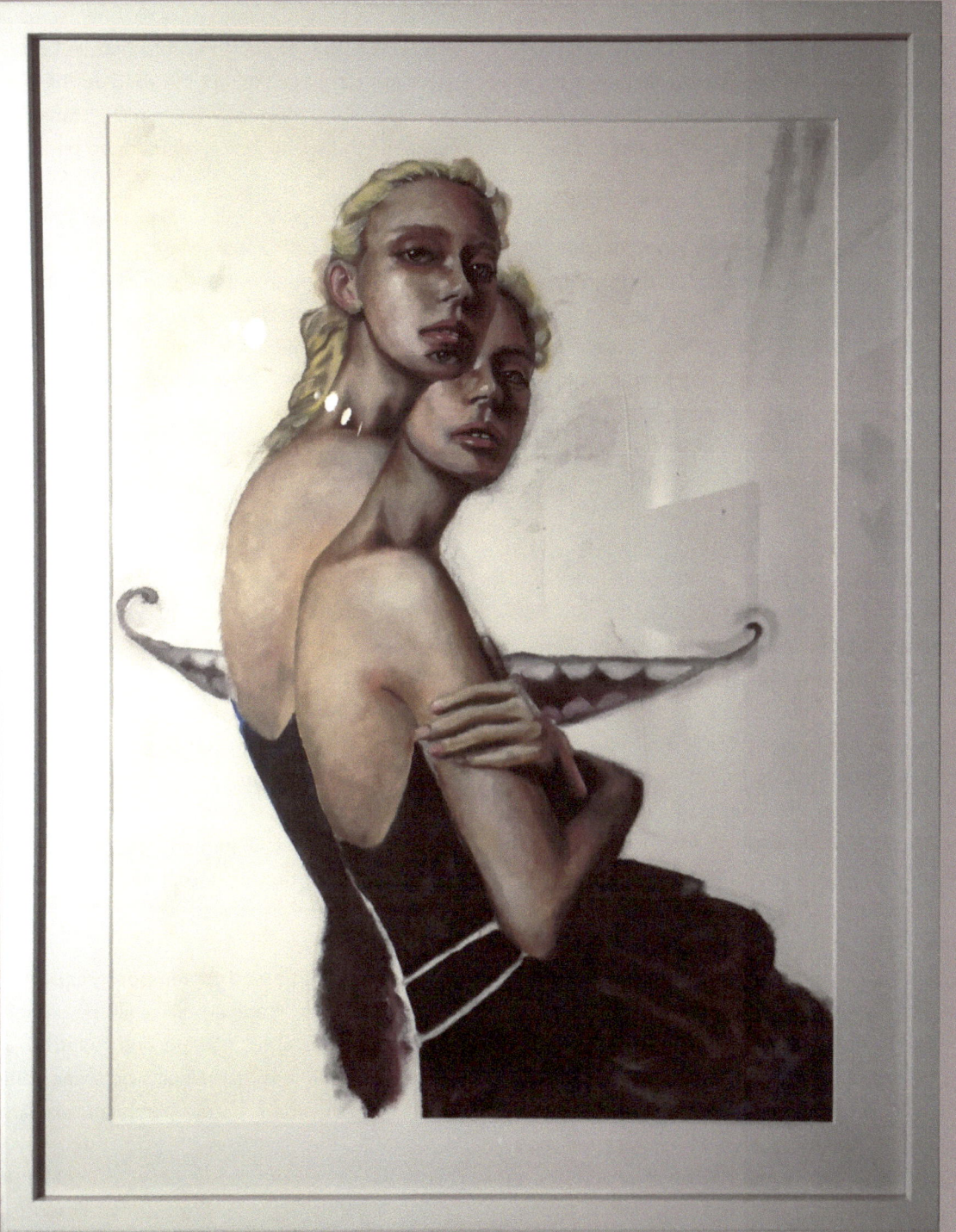

In Two | oil on gesso paper | 22.5 x 28.5 inches

Brandon Breaux is a multidisciplinary artist and art director born in an working from Chicago. His work utilizes the mediums oil painting, video, graphic design, fashion design, interactive and installation design, with oil painting being his art practice's primary focus. Brandon is currently producing and sharing work in solo and group shows

Myia Brown is a Chicago native whose work focuses on the internal struggles of a person that can extend to the world around them. Being the 5th of 6 children has unconsciously developed her love of individualism and the desire to learn personality development in relation to social interactions. Her BA in Studio Art from Saint Xavier University continues to help her ambitions in various forms of art such as drawing, painting, video, and sculpture. Myia is currently freelancing in the Chicago area.

Lee Bullitt is a Fine Art photographer living and working in Brooklyn. Her photographs maintain a narrative quality that often feel as if the viewers are taking an intimate look at seemingly private, infinitely emotional moments in time.

Daniel Gamez is a photographer born and raised in Chicago, Illinois, where he currently resides. His interest in photography began in the middle of his high school career, Robert Lindblom Math & Science Academy. Mr. Nathan Diamond, Daniel's homeroom and art teacher introduced him to analog photography in 2007. By the summer of 2009, Daniel was heading to Columbia College Chicago with a photography internship at Gallery 37 Center for the Arts.

Later that internship would become Daniel first teaching opportunity, as co-instructor working along side Mr. Paul Jones who helped Daniel furthers his passion and skill for analog photography. Graduating from Columbia College Chicago in December of 2014 with a Bachelor of Arts in Photography, with a concentration in Fine Art. His main body of work, "Homeless, Please Help" causes the viewer to interact with people who happen to be homeless for one reason or another.

As Daniel went about his daily routine, he realized that for some reason he had begun to ignore people living on the street. He was avoiding eye contact but reading the sign that the people created. After talking with friends, Daniel was not alone in creating this social pattern of ignoring people's pleas for help.

"Homeless, Please Help" was created using a 19th century printing process called cyanotype. Daniel took these portraits using his medium format camera, printing on the subject's respective sign. Daniel wants to recreate social interaction between those asking for help and the people who may/or may not respond.

David Anthony Geary is a multidisciplinary artist working in a variety of mediums for the last 20 years. His work incorporates painting, printmaking, collage, assemblage, sculpture or photography. The nuance of the human experience, both the introspective and observed are an integral part of his process. With a practice of visual study New Orleans, LA at Xavier University.

Culture and life experiences fill his work along with the discovery of newness. Constantly pushing, searching and discovering the new while at the same time holding on to the old. It's not just an aspect of David's art but an aspect of his character that finds its way into the art. Communicating his perspective of the world around him through a visual language, he became fluent in many dialects of visual art.

Reisha, Chicago based contemporary fine art photographer and painter, creates images, holistically by combining conception, styling, photography, collage and found objects . For several years, Reisha has sustained both an artistic and erotic investigation into the nature of human sexuality.

Reisha's first major body of work, coffee table book *Sexy Clowns* published in 2012 presents a satirical body of images that pose as a commentary on stereotypical ideas of women's sexuality. Showcasing approximately 116 pages of photographs of women in a variety of "everyday scenarios exaggerated by risqué clothing and garish clown make up. The book highlights sexuality, fashion, make-up and social political introspection.

Reisha is currently co-owner of Galleryna19 and has also expanded her artistic efforts into the world of mixed media, specifically intricate collage works. Her use of unique and textured paper creates mind boggling effects on viewers.

Victoria Selbach is a New York Contemporary Realist best known for her lifesize nude depictions of women caught at the intersection of light and shadow. Her gaze is directed through a deep connection to individuals who carry their strong presence and beauty into her paintings. Capturing the intricacies of unique women through a powerful merging of empathy and paint allows Selbach to deepen her understanding of herself and promotes a journey to uncover and embrace the diversity and complexity of all the women we are. Selbachs work has exhibited nationally, including the Heckscher Museum of Art, The Butler Institute of American Art and the Tullman Art Collection. *The Huffington Post* reviewed Selbach's work in an article by Priscilla Frank, 'Finally, Artist Paints Female Nudes As They Really Are'. An archive of Selbachs work is available at victoriaselbach.com.

Saba Taj is a mixed-media visual artist and activist from North Carolina. Her work explores American Muslim identity and challenges the current climate of Islamophobia by creating hybridized images that offer an alternative to monolithic representations of Muslim women.

Martha A. Wade is a visual artist from Chicago who has always carried a deep passion for art making. Her painting style utilizes whimsical themes of fantasy and hope, to portray cultural and historical themes in a positive tone. Her artwork has a dreamlike feel, as Martha works to create a sense of movement in every piece.

You will often find star constellations hidden in Martha's work - her way of visualizing that we are all made of stardust. Her art seeks to uplift spirits by giving a glimpse of what people can achieve at our highest potential. Her tapestry of everyday people with rustic elements of fantasy suggest that common ground exists, where everyone is empowered to fulfill their dreams.

Martha's work often has a dual theme, as in her series of children with spirit animals of Childhood Dreams & Conquered Fears. The message speaks to the strength of children who are often fearless, and at the same time encourages us to hold on to our innocence. Her latest body of work Sirens deals with the blessings and stigma of being a powerful woman, often seen as intimidating and alluring by others.

Martha learned to create at the foot of her artist father Eugene "Eda" Wade, who she watched and admired as a young girl longing for a canvas of her own. She has gone on to create over 200 paintings on wood and canvas. Her work can be found in private homes and collections around the world. She is a member of the NextGen 75 Board of the South Side Community Arts Center, and striving to empower younger generations to get involved in the arts. Martha is co-owner of Galleryna19, a fine art gallery in the Oak Park Arts District showcasing contemporary work.

Guanyu Xu (b.1993 Beijing) is studying for BFA degree in the School of the Art Institute of Chicago. He was the recipient of the Fred Endsley Memorial Fellowship and the finalist of Lucie Foundation Emerging Artist Scholarship. His works have been exhibited internationally including the Center for Fine Art Photography, Fort Collins; New York Photo Festival, New York; Orange County Center for Contemporary Art, Santa Ana; Embassy Tea Gallery, London; Ph21 Gallery, Budapest, and others. His works have been featured in numerous publications including *AintBad Magazine*, *ArtAscent* and *China Photographic Publishing House*.

PoetsArtists

GOSS183 Publishing House | Bloomington, Illinois

www.poetsandartists.com | Issue #76

All Rights Reserved ©2016.

Publisher / Editor / Creator Didi Menendez